For Will, Al, Len and Ivy,
Keep making the future exciting

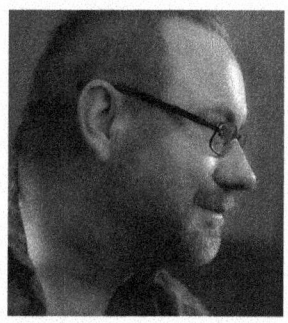

Mike Bonsall has spent way too much time creating digital ghosts of Ballard's work. He was the first to create an online concordance of a living author; turned *High-Rise* into a cartoon; tracked down the location of *Concrete Island*; created the 'original' text of 'The Index'; made the *Crash* test dummies speak; turned *The Terminal Beach* into an interactive text game; created not one but three Ballard-Bots; made an infinite cut-up of *The Atrocity Exhibition,* and set up a Ballard AI that churned out bad pastiche. More evidence at digital-ballard.com

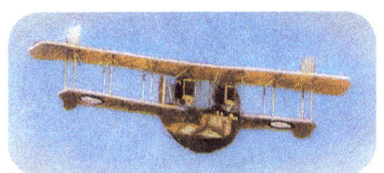

Ballardian Diversions

Mike Bonsall

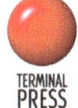

TERMINAL PRESS

Ballardian Diversions

ISBN: 978-1-990682-12-4

First Edition

Published By
THE TERMINAL PRESS
Powell River, BC, Canada

Text and images copyright © 2025 Mike Bonsall
except book cover images which retain original copyright.
All rights reserved.

Mike Bonsall photo by Tim Chapman
Back Cover photo by Rick McGrath

No part of this book may be reproduced by any means, in any media, electronic or mechanical, including motion picture film, video, photocopy, recording, or any other information storage retrieval system, without prior permission in writing from the publisher and author. Any use of this publication to "train" generative artificial intelligence (AI) technologies to generate text is expressly prohibited. So there.

Contents

JG Ballard In The Dissecting Room
PAGE 11

Mind-Mapping "The Terminal Beach"
PAGE 35

Deep Learning with JG Ballard
PAGE 48

Ballard in Legoland
PAGE 60

The Bonsall/Ballard Terminal Tarot
PAGE 72

JG Ballard's Book of Knowledge
PAGE 98

Development Of High-Rise: The Model
PAGE 112

Ballard Bots
PAGE 120

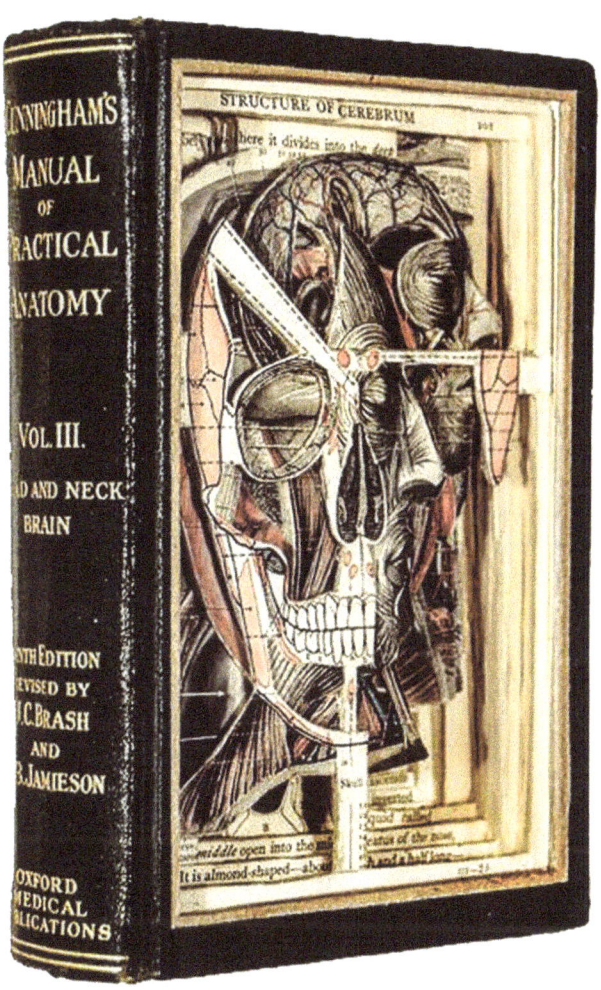

JG Ballard in the Dissecting Room

Illustration: *Cunningham's Manual of Practical Anatomy Volume III. Head, Neck and Brain* by Brian Dettmer

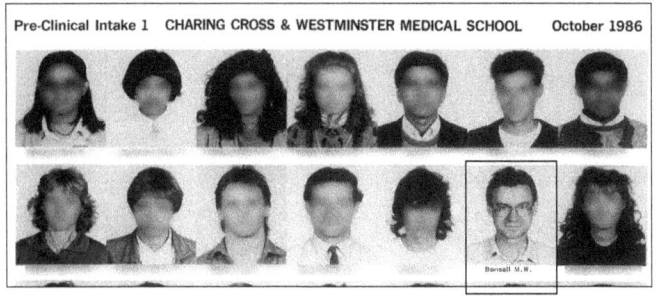

From October 1949 to 1951 J.G. Ballard studied medicine at Cambridge, studying anatomy, physiology and biochemistry before he would be allowed to touch a living patient.

I had a similar experience of medical school—from October 1986 to 1988 I studied medicine at Charing Cross and Westminster medical school. My own first visit to the dissecting room felt unreal. The rows of corpses not just unmoving but somehow unhuman. Completely unnerved by this exhibition of death, I screamed soundlessly at my legs to walk to the exit, never to come back. But I was frozen by fear, knowing it wasn't possible to go back. Ballard's dissecting room seems to have been in some kind of cellar, while mine was the 'penthouse' of the *High-Rise* that is Charing Cross Hospital, with magnificent views over the Thames—but mostly we were turned inwards.

Like Ballard I had a female cadaver to dissect, tied into a muslin tube, a label attached to her big toe like in a cheap gangster film. The name on that label I can still remember thirty years later. We six students firstly had to extract her from this cloth pupa so we could start her lengthy journey to flayed butterfly. It was sobering to realise our dissection guides were practical documents rather than science fiction.

I used my clumsy scalpel to make that first cut into the hardened skin below her shrunken breasts and eventually removed them completely to allow access to her chest wall. Later—a dark dissecting room joke—I would say to my male colleagues; 'Wouldn't it be horrible, if the first time we saw a naked woman, we had to cut her tits off?'

From their reactions I could tell this had been the first time they had seen a naked woman.

It is typical of Ballard's sublime imagination that he was able to transform the grisly process of dissection into an apotheosis. As well as the student pranks and black humour of the dissection room, we also had a passionate care for our cadavers. I can still remember the tortuous process of opening our cadaver's skull and the feeling of awe at holding her brain in my hands. As we gradually examined and cut away each part of our body, the discarded parts were placed into a large steel bin, one bin per cadaver—it was a matter of honour always to put your body parts in the right bin.

At the end of our ministrations, these scraps would be bundled together and buried. We students were encouraged to attend the end-of-year church service where our cadavers were finally laid to rest, though I managed to avoid that ritual.

Perhaps the last time Mrs. A. was cared for as a human being, a plaster was placed in the crook of her left arm, possibly after a last blood sample was taken. Despite all our other decrements, we found ourselves unable to simply rip that plaster off, or even touch it.

Eventually we defused this talisman of our own death by cutting the skin around it and removing the whole block of skin from under it.

Like Ballard I had a dissection manual, a minutely detailed guide to the two-year process of dismantling the human form. Like his, mine was soon stained with human fat and formalin preservative. The acrid smell of formaldehyde became a central part of my life, leaching deep into the skin of my hands. The wearing of gloves was frowned on; "You have to be able to feel your way about inside the body..." The smell was with me as I ate a sandwich for lunch, and with me at night, stronger than the scent of my partner. After a while I no longer cared if there were parts of Mrs. A. under my fingernails.

Several times Ballard mentions that his dissection guide was *Cunningham's*. Ballard would have used the eleventh edition of *Cunningham's Manual of Practical Anatomy* which was published from 1948 to 1952. I got hold of copies of all of the three volumes of this edition. With its precise, matter-of-fact technical language, partnered with the most extraordinary images of human dismemberment—drawn with unflinching accuracy from cadavers in the dissecting room—it gives some insight into Ballard's experiences at the time.

Ballard's work is indeed suffused with the language and terminology of the dissecting room, sometimes obviously, as in *Crash*, but sometimes the very landscape is described in anatomical terms, external reality quantified in terms of internal spaces.

What follows are some examples of the way Ballard reworked his early anatomical experience into a new kind of fiction, together with some of the words and images from the *Cunningham's Manual* that might have settled into his uniquely fertile teenage mind.

> "At the end of his opening lecture Harris warned that a small number of us would be unable to cope with the sight of the cadavers waiting for dissection on the glass-topped tables. Walking into that strange, low-ceilinged chamber, halfway between a nightclub and an abattoir, was an unnerving experience. The cadavers, greenish-yellow with formaldehyde, lay naked on their backs, their skins covered with scars and contusions, and seemed barely human, as if they had just been taken down from a Grunewald Crucifixion. Several students in my group dropped out, unable to cope with the sight of their first dead bodies, but in many ways the experience of dissection was just as overwhelming for me"
>
> J.G. Ballard, *Miracles of Life*

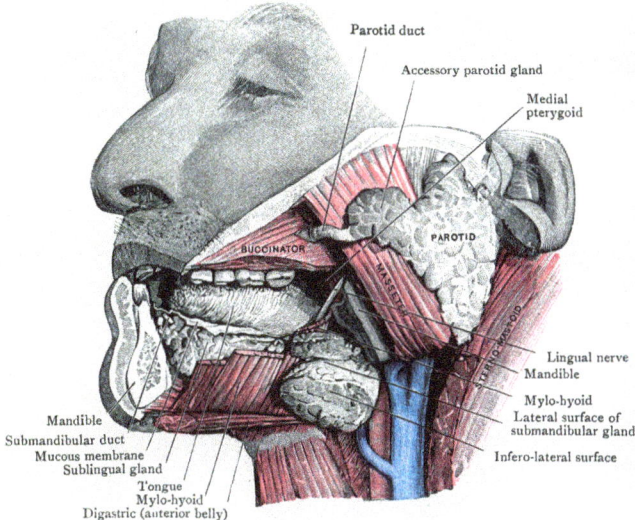

Fig. 72.—Dissection of Parotid, Submandibular and Sublingual Glands.

"Looking at the contents of the cabin as he sipped his drink, Ransom debated which of his possessions to take with him. The cabin had become, unintentionally, a repository of all the talismans of his life. On the bookshelf were the anatomy texts he had used in the dissecting room as a student, the pages stained with the formalin that leaked from the corpses on the tables, somewhere among them the unknown face of his surgeon father." (*The Drought*, 1965)

ABDOMEN

WHEN the body is brought into the dissecting-room, it may be placed first in the " lithotomy position " and retained in that position for three days, during which time the dissectors of the Abdomen dissect the *perineum*. The dissection of the

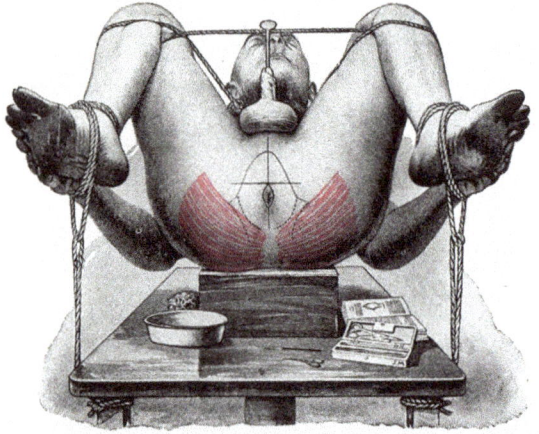

FIG. 76.—Body in "lithotomy position", showing the boundaries of the Perineum and the skin incisions. The position of the Gluteus Maximus is indicated in red.

"The volumes of Helen's thighs pressing against my hips, her left fist buried in my shoulder, her mouth grasping at my own, the shape and moisture of her anus as I stroked it with my ring finger, were each overlaid by the inventories of a benevolent technology—the moulded binnacle of the instrument dials, the jutting carapace of the steering column shroud, the extravagant pistol grip of the handbrake. I felt the warm vinyl of the seat beside me, and then stroked the damp aisle of Helen's perineum. Her hand pressed against my right testicle. The plastic laminates around me, the colour of washed anthracite, were the same tones as her pubic hairs parted at the vestibule of her vulva. The passenger compartment enclosed us like a machine generating from our sexual act an homunculus of blood, semen and engine coolant. My finger moved into Helen's rectum, feeling the shaft of my penis within her vagina. These slender membranes, like the mucous septum of her nose which I touched with my tongue, were reflected in the glass dials of the instrument panel, the unbroken curve of the windshield." (*Crash*, 1973)

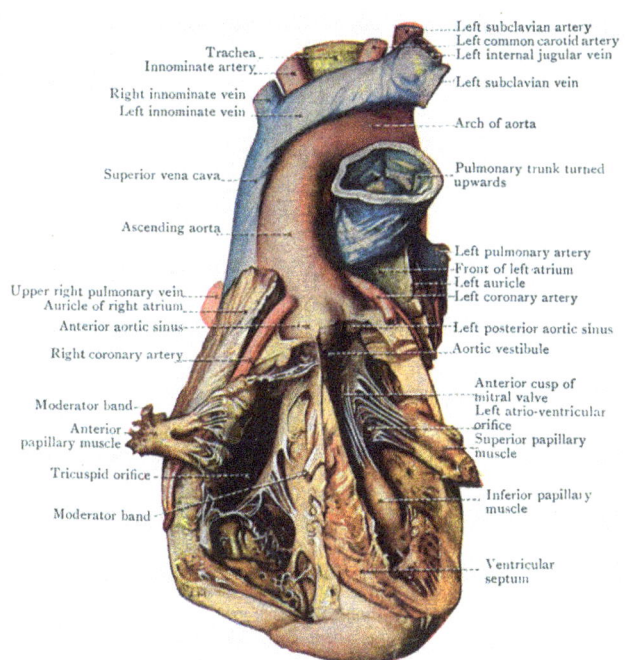

Fig. 54.—Dissection of Ventricles of Heart. The pulmonary trunk has been separated from the infundibulum of the right ventricle and turned up to show the root of the aorta.

"'Of course.' Jim reflected on all this as he walked to the hospital. He often watched the eyes of the patients as they died, trying to detect a flash of light when the soul left. Once he had helped Dr Ransome as he massaged the naked chest of a young Belgian woman wasted by dysentery. Dr Bowen had said that she was dead, but Dr Ransome squeezed her heart under her ribs and suddenly her eyes swivelled and looked at Jim. At first Jim thought that her soul had returned to her, but she was still dead. Mrs. Philips and Mrs Gilmour took her away and buried her an hour later. Dr Ransome explained that for a few seconds he had pumped the blood back into her brain." (*Empire of the Sun*, 1984)

PLATE VII

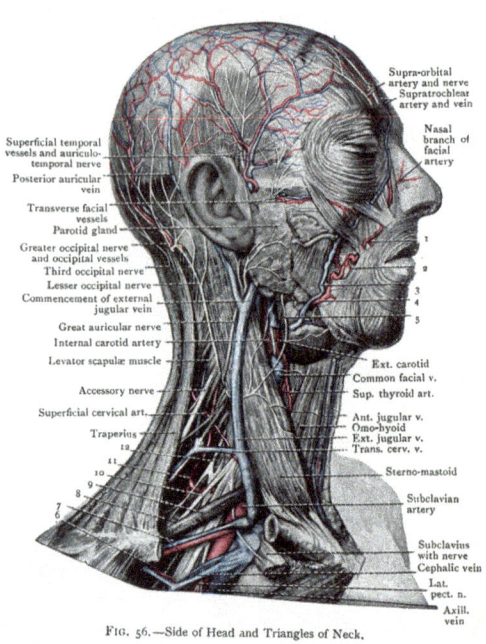

FIG. 56.—Side of Head and Triangles of Neck.

"'Relax, Karen.' In a mimicry of Dr Nathan's voice, he added, 'You're a mere modulus, my dear.' He looked down at the translucent skin over the anterior triangle of her neck, barely hiding its scenarios of nerve and blood-vessel. Marker lines sped past them, dividing and turning. The helicopter waited below the ruined control tower. He pulled her from the car, then buttoned his flying jacket around her shoulders." ("The Great American Nude", 1967)

"Even that morning's swim in the lagoon had failed to clear his head. Neil gripped his thighs, trying to steady the sweating muscles that still jumped in a fever of their own. The effort of spear-fishing in the lagoon each day had leached all the fat from his skin, and the strings of his muscles reminded him of the anatomical plates in his father's textbooks, the skin flayed back to expose the knotted cords and straps." (*Rushing to Paradise*, 1994)

shaped like a crescent moon. It rounds off the apex of the pubic arch, and its horns extend for some distance along the inferior rami of the pubic bones. An oval aperture that transmits the deep dorsal vein of the penis (or clitoris) separates it from the transverse ligament of the perineum.

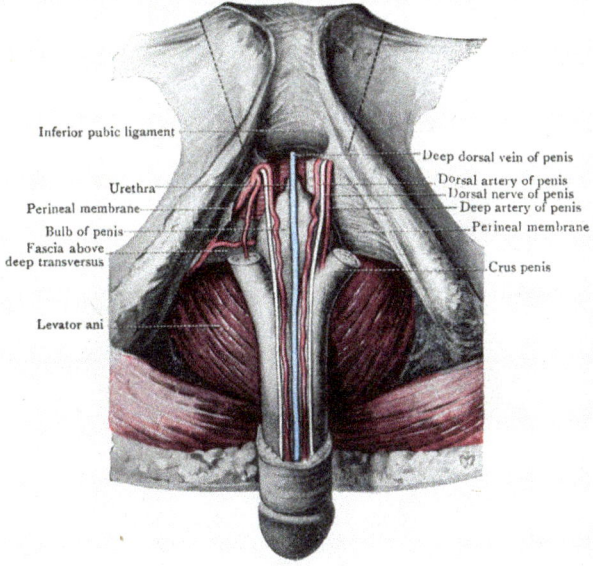

FIG. 213.—Dissection to show Pubic Symphysis and Dorsal Vessels and Nerves of Penis. The dotted lines indicate the saw-cuts required in the alternative dissection mentioned on p. 403.

"I laid my penis at the mouth of his rectum. His anus opened around the head of my penis, settling itself around the shaft, his hard detrusor muscles gripping my glans. As I moved in and out of his rectum the lightborne vehicles soaring along the motorway drew the semen from my testicles. After my orgasm I lifted myself slowly from Vaughan, holding his buttocks apart with my hands so as not to injure his rectum. Still parting his buttocks, I watched my semen leak from his anus across the fluted ribbing of the vinyl upholstery." (*Crash*, 1973)

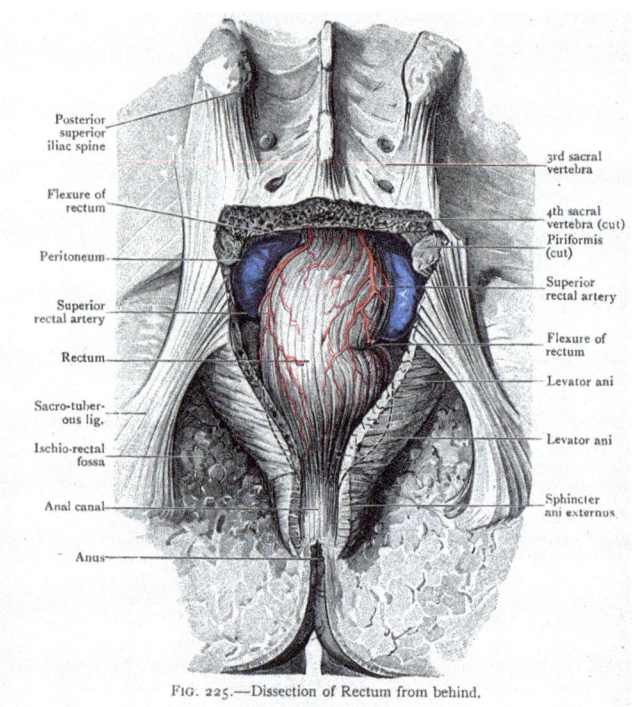

FIG. 225.—Dissection of Rectum from behind.

"She knelt on the carpet, her chest and shoulders across the cushions. Spitting on her fingers, she pushed the saliva into her anus with one hand, testing my penis with the other. I hesitated to enter her, nervous of tearing her scarred anus, but she pressed my penis into her, adding more spit between the gasps of pain. When I was fully inside her she at last relaxed, and her rectum was as soft as the vagina of a child-bearing woman. She buried her face among the teddy bears and brought her wrists behind her back, inviting me to force them to her shoulder blades. I moved carefully, trying to control her prolapsing rectum, gently forcing her arms as she wanted, picking the hairs from her mouth as she shouted to me, an eager, desperate child.

'Bugger me, daddy! Beat me! Pixie wants to be buggered!'"(*The Kindness of Women*, 1991)

anterior descend under cover of the plexus, between it and the scalenus medius.

Anteriorly, a large number of structures intervene between the plexus and the skin :—(1) The superficial fascia contain-

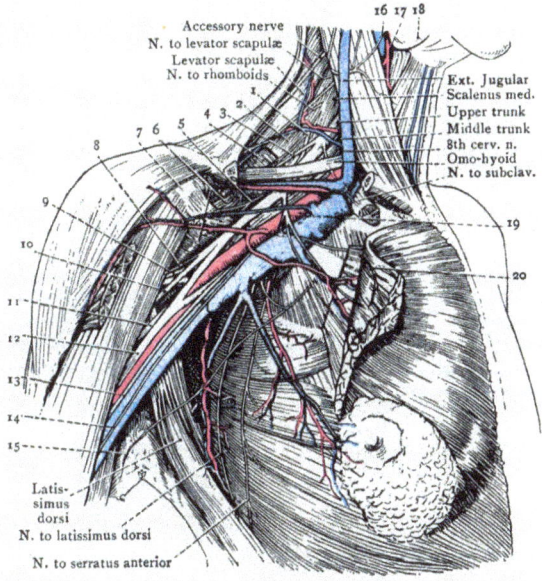

FIG. 16.—Dissection to show the General Relations of the Brachial Plexus.

"'Not in our minds, Robert. These are the oldest memories on Earth, the time-codes carried in every chromosome and gene. Every step we've taken in our evolution is a milestone inscribed with organic memories—from the enzymes controlling the carbon dioxide cycle to the organisation of the brachial plexus and the nerve pathways of the Pyramid cells in the mid-brain, each is a record of a thousand decisions taken in the face of a sudden physico-chemical crisis. Just as psychoanalysis reconstructs the original traumatic situation in order to release the repressed material, so we are now being plunged back into the archaeopsychic past, uncovering the ancient taboos and drives that have been dormant for epochs...'" (*The Drowned World*, 1962)

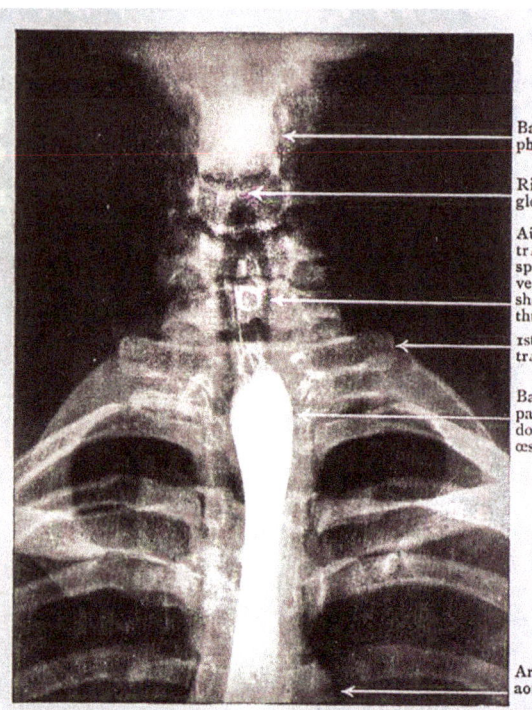

FIG. 110 B.—Antero-posterior Radiograph of Neck and upper part of Thorax of young woman as "barium paste" is swallowed (Dr. R. McWhirter). Note the deviation of the œsophagus to the left.

"Captain Webster studied the prints. They showed: (1) a thick-set man in an Air Force jacket, unshaven face half hidden by the dented hat-peak; (2) a transverse section through the spinal level T-12; (3) a crayon self-portrait by David Feary, seven-year-old schizophrenic at the Belmont Asylum, Sutton; (4) radio-spectra from the quasar CTA 102; (5) an antero-posterior radiograph of a skull, estimated capacity 1500 cc; (6) spectro-heliogram of the sun taken with the K line of calcium; (7) left and right handprints showing massive scarring between second and third metacarpal bones. To Dr Nathan he said, 'And all these make up one picture?'" ("You and Me and the Continuum", 1966)

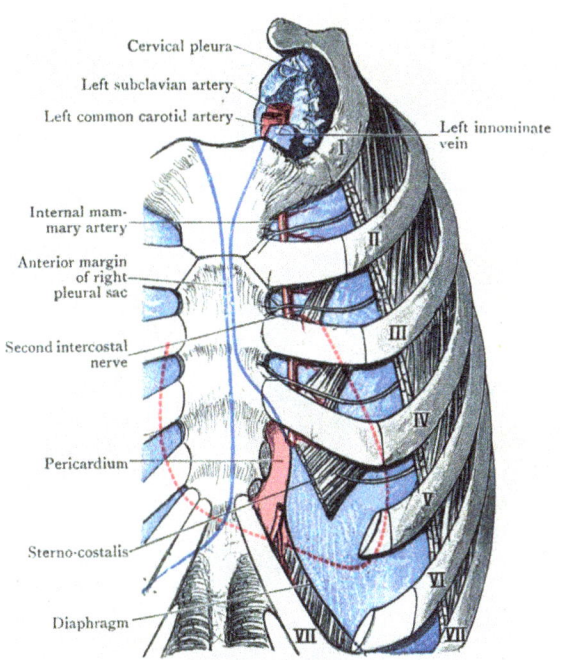

FIG. 12.—Diagram to show the Parts in front of Pericardium and Heart. The outline of the heart is indicated in red by a dotted line, and the anterior margins of the pleural sacs are represented by blue lines.

"Already sweating in the humid air, Mallory returned to the bedroom. Anne had woken, but lay motionless in the centre of the bed, strands of blonde hair caught like a child's in her mouth. With its fixed and empty expression, her face resembled a clock that had just stopped. Mallory sat down and placed his hands on her diaphragm, gently respiring her. Every morning he feared that time would run out for Anne while she slept, leaving her forever in the middle of a last uneasy dream." (*Memories of the Space Age*, 1982)

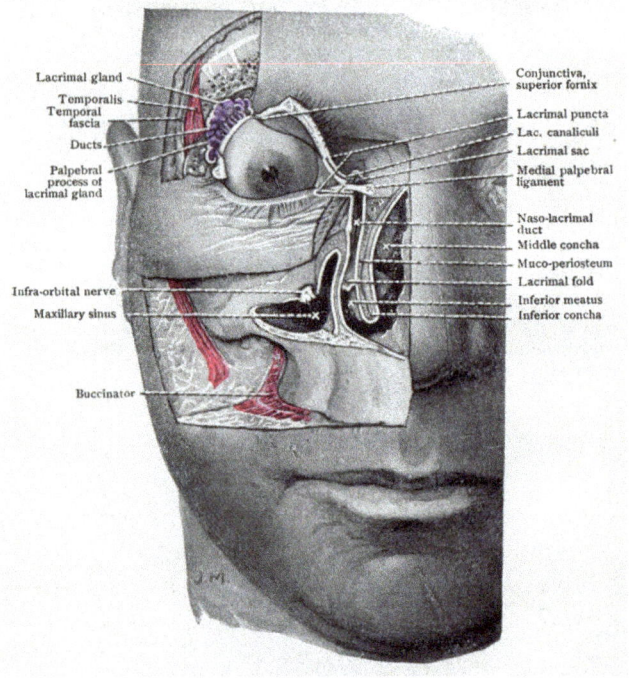

Clean the medial palpebral ligament, and identify the *lacrimal sac*, which lies behind it. Note the lacrimal part of the orbicularis oculi as it curves forwards round the lateral side of the sac.

"Tasting blood in his mouth, he stopped and sat down. Squatting on the powdery slope, he took the handkerchief from his pocket and touched his tongue and lips. The red stain formed the imprint of his shaky mouth, like an illicit kiss. Maitland felt the tender skin of his right temple and cheekbone. The bruise ran from the ear as far as his right nostril. Pressing a finger into the nasal cleft, he could feel the injured sinus and gums, a loosened eye-tooth." (*Concrete Island*, 1974)

"These deaths preoccupied Travers… Jacqueline Kennedy: the notional death, defined by the exquisite eroticism of her mouth and the logic of her leg stance; Buddy Holly: the capped teeth of the dead pop singer, like the melancholy dolmens of the Brittany coastline, were globes of milk, condensations of his sleeping mind. ("Tolerances of the Human Face", 1969)

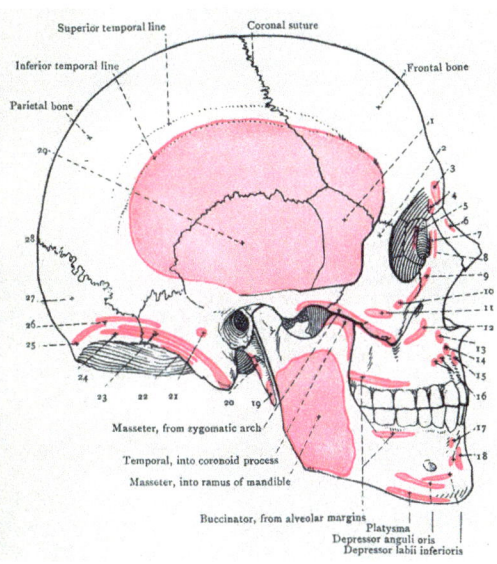

"**Waking:** the concrete embankment of a motorway extension. Roadworks, cars drumming two hundred yards below. In the sunlight the seams between the sections are illuminated like the sutures of an exposed skull. A young woman stands ten feet away from him, watching with unsure eyes. The hyoid bone in her throat flutters as if discharging some subvocal rosary. She points to her car, parked off the verge beside a grader, and then beckons to him. Kline, Coma, Xero. He remembered the aloof, cerebral Kline and their long discussions on this terminal concrete beach. Under a different sun. This girl is not Coma. 'My car.' She speaks, the sounds as dissociated as the recording in a doll. 'I can give you a lift. I saw you reach the island. It's like trying to cross the Styx.'" ("The Assassination Weapon", 1966)

"A faded agency picture of the car in which Albert Camus had died was elaborately re-worked, the dashboard and windshield marked with the words 'nasal bridge', 'soft palate', 'left zygomatic arch'. An area in the lower section of the instrument panel was reserved for Camus' genital organs, the dials covered with cross-hatching and provided at the left margin with a key: 'glans penis', 'scrotal septum', 'urethral canal', 'right testicle.'" (*Crash*, 1973)

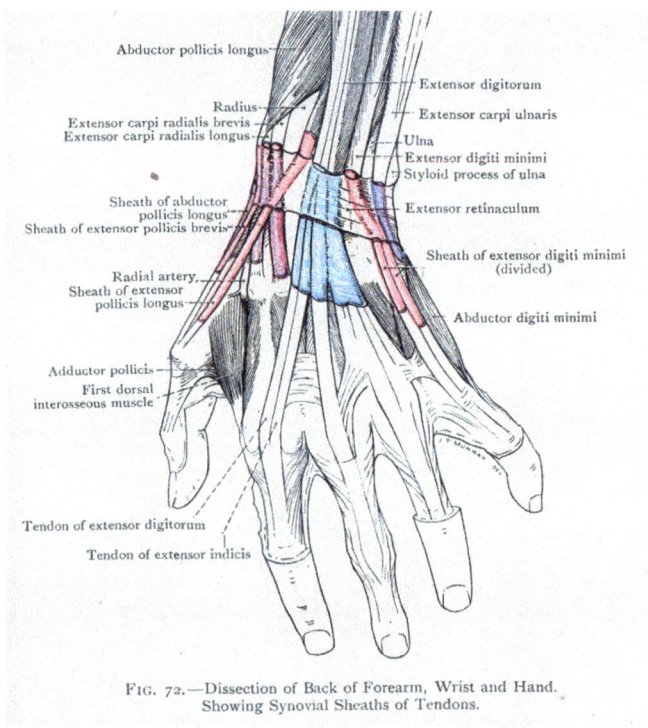

FIG. 72.—Dissection of Back of Forearm, Wrist and Hand. Showing Synovial Sheaths of Tendons.

"Tallis was immediately struck by the unusual planes of her face, intersecting each other like the dunes around her. When she offered him a cigarette he involuntarily held her wrist, feeling the junction between the radius and ulna bones. He followed her across the dunes. The young woman was a geometric equation, the demonstration model of a landscape. Her breasts and buttocks illustrated Enneper's surface of negative constant curve, the differential coefficient of the pseudo-sphere." ("You: Coma: Marilyn Monroe", 1966)

"'Doctor ...' Kagwa's strong hand gripped my right elbow, his fingers deliberately bruising the ulna nerve. He closed the cell door on the soldier, who had placed the mess-tin on the floor beside the European and was about to remove the slops bucket. 'Your duties now are complete. You may return to your clinic and finish your packing.'" (*The Day of Creation*, 1987)

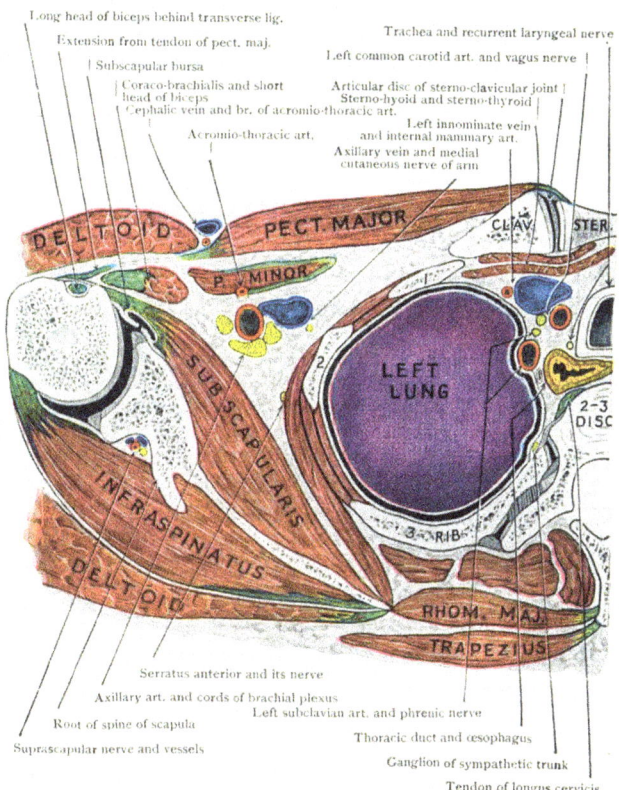

FIG. 11.—Horizontal Section at the level of Shoulder Joint
(based on a section by Symington).
The chief structures in the Axilla and its Walls are shown, and also
the chief relations of the Left Sterno-Clavicular Joint.

"The white flanks of the dunes reminded him of the endless promenades of Karen Novotny's body—diorama of flesh and hillock; the broad avenues of the thighs, piazzas of pelvis and abdomen, the closed arcades of the womb. This terracing of Karen's body in the landscape of the beach in some way diminished the identity of the young woman asleep in her apartment. He walked among the displaced contours of her pectoral girdle. What time could be read off the slopes and inclines of this inorganic musculature, the drifting planes of its face? ("You: Coma: Marilyn Monroe", 1966)

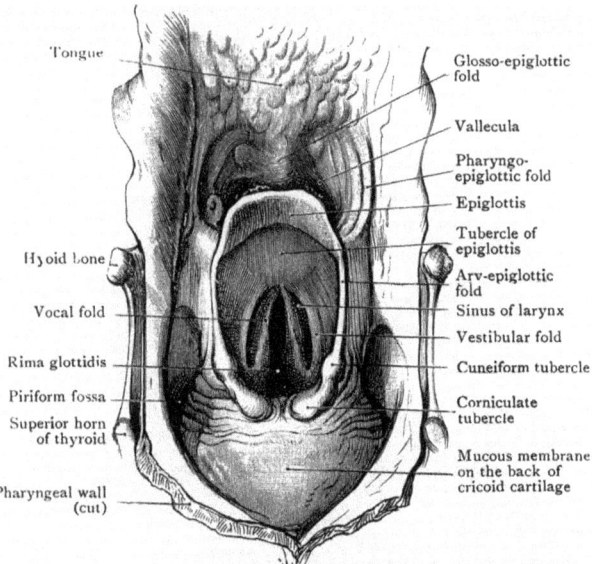

FIG. 112.—Anterior Wall of Laryngeal Part of Pharynx.

"Lang was lying in his cot, body motionless under the canvas sheet. His lips were parted slightly. No sound came from them but Morley, bending over next to Neill, could see his hyoid bone vibrating in spasms.

'He's very faint,' the intern warned." ("Manhole 69", 1957)

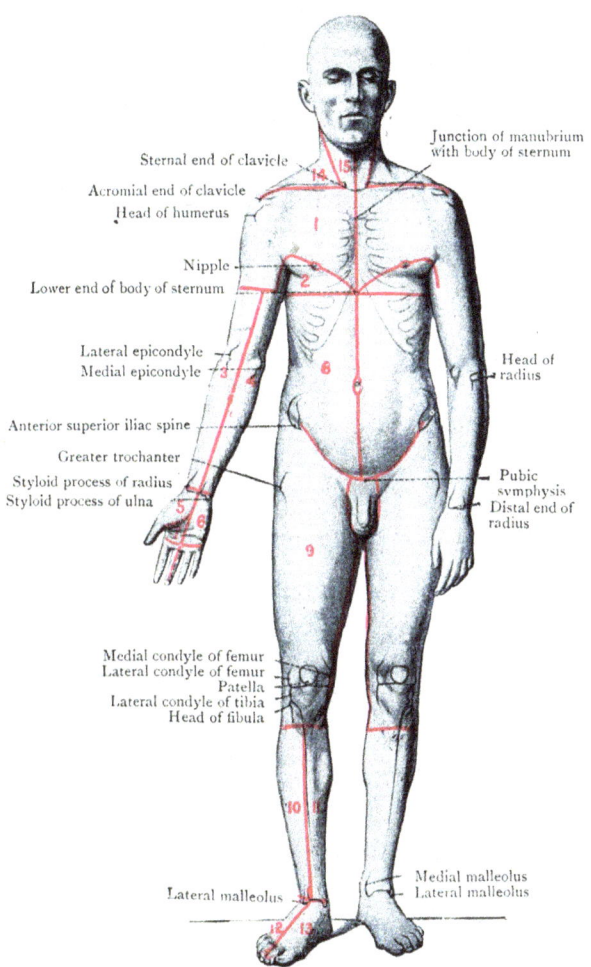

FIG. 91.—Landmarks and Incisions.

"After a year at London University I was thrown out of the medical school—while dissecting a thorax in the anatomy laboratory one afternoon I suddenly became convinced that the cadaver was still alive. I terrorized a weak fellow student into helping me to frogmarch the corpse up and down the laboratory in an attempt to revive it. I am still half-certain that we would have succeeded." (*The Unlimited Dream Company*, 1979)

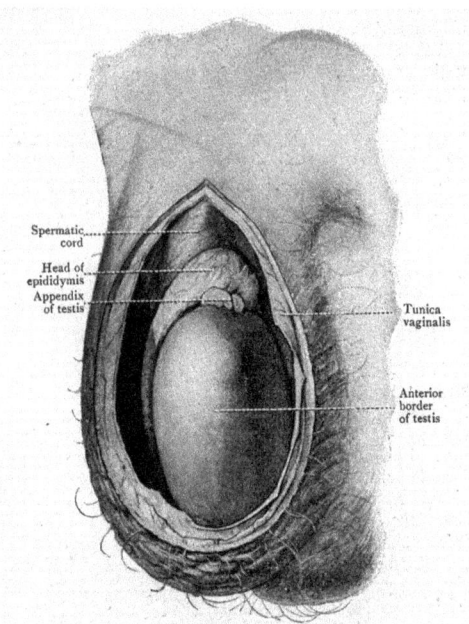

FIG. 106.—Right Testis and Epididymis within Tunica Vaginalis exposed by removal of anterior wall of scrotum.

"One recalls Goethe's notion that the skull is formed of modified vertebrae—similarly, the bones of the pelvis may constitute the remains of a lost sacral skull. The resemblance between histologies of lung and kidney has long been noted. Other correspondences of respiratory and urinogenital function come to mind, enshrined both in popular mythology (the supposed equivalence in size of nose and penis) and psychoanalytic symbolism (the "eyes" are a common code for the testicles). In conclusion, it seems that Travis's extreme sensitivity to the volumes and geometry of the world around him, and their immediate translation into psychological terms, may reflect a belated attempt to return to a symmetrical world, one that will recapture the perfect symmetry of the blastosphere, and the acceptance of the "Mythology of the Amniotic Return". In his mind World War III represents the final self-destruction and imbalance of an asymmetric world. The human organism is an atrocity exhibition at which he is an unwilling spectator ..."' (*The Atrocity Exhibition*, 1966)

PLATE XXIV

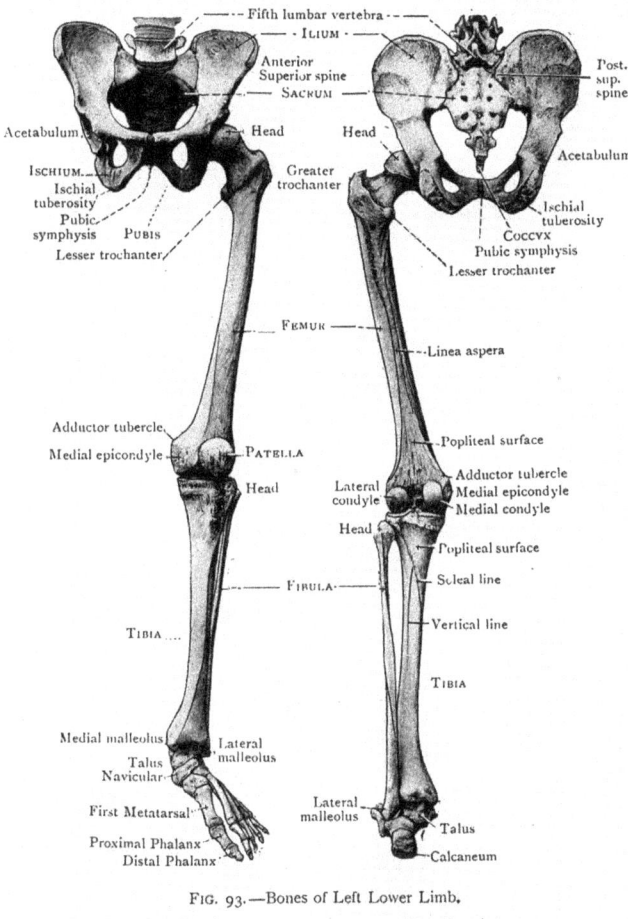

FIG. 93.—Bones of Left Lower Limb.

Anterior view. Posterior view.

"The remainder of the skeleton, stripped of all flesh, still rests on the sea shore, the clutter of bleached ribs like the timbers of a derelict ship. The contractor's hut, the crane and the scaffolding have been removed, and the sand being driven into the bay along the coast has buried the pelvis and backbone. In the winter the high curved bones are deserted, battered by the breaking waves, but in the summer they provide an excellent perch for the sea-wearying gulls." ("The Drowned Giant", 1964)

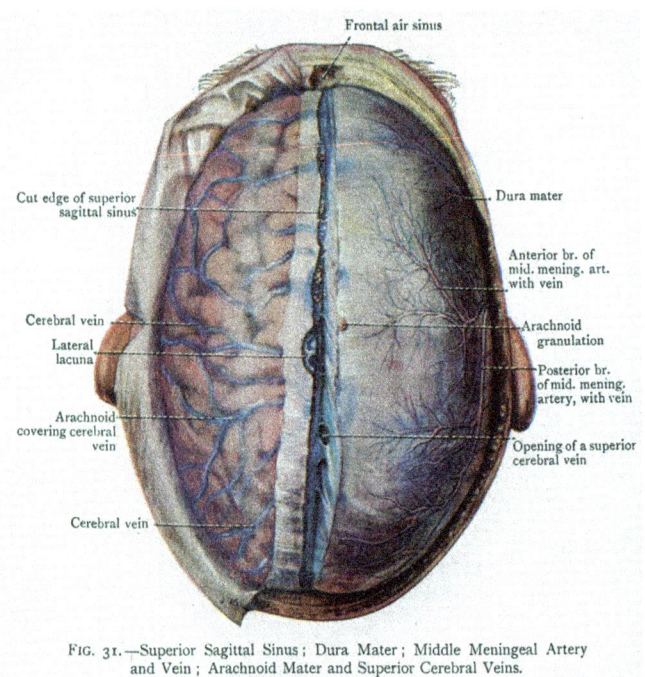

FIG. 31.—Superior Sagittal Sinus; Dura Mater; Middle Meningeal Artery and Vein; Arachnoid Mater and Superior Cerebral Veins.

"Larsen nodded, sipping his whisky. 'You're suggesting that the hallucination was a mental flashback?'

"'Precisely. The stream of retinal images reaching the optic lobe is nothing more than a film strip. Every image is stored away, thousands of reels, a hundred thousand hours of running time. Usually flashbacks are deliberate, when we consciously select a few blurry stills from the film library, a childhood scene, the image of our neighbourhood streets we carry around with us all day near the surface of consciousness. But upset the projector slightly—overstrain could do it—jolt it back a few hundred frames, and you'll superimpose a completely irrelevant strip of already exposed film, in your case a glimpse of yourself sitting on the sofa. It's the apparent irrelevancy that is so frightening.'" ("Zone of Terror", 1960)

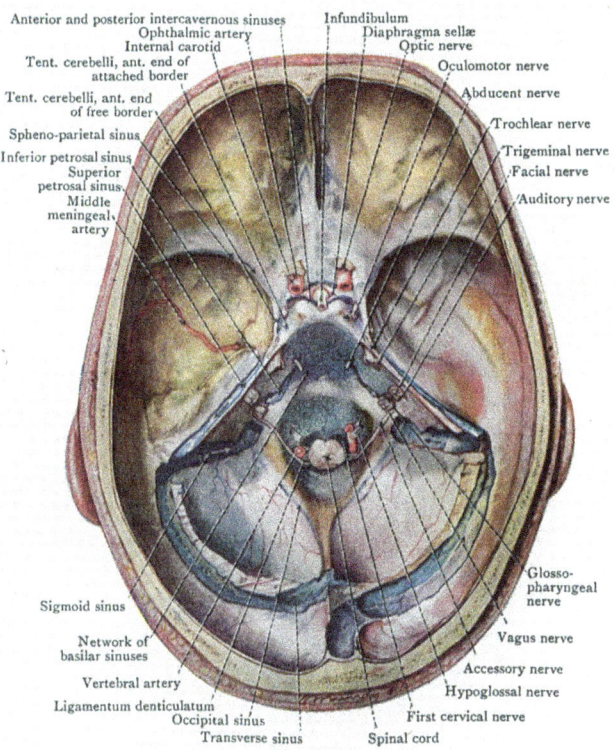

Fig. 43.—Dissection of the Floor of the Cranial Cavity after removal of the Brain.

"Like to try a really new sort of dream? The Set Corrani Priests of Theta Piscium will link you up with the sacred electronic thought-pools in the Desert of Kish. These mercury lakes are their ancestral memory banks. Surgery is necessary but be careful. Too much cortical damage and the archetypes may get restive. In return one of the Set Corrani (polysexual delta-humanoids about the size of a walking dragline) will take over your cerebral functions for a long weekend. All these transactions are done on an exchange basis and SLEEP TRADERS charge nothing for the service. But they obviously get a rake-off, and may pump advertising into the lower medullary centres. Whatever they're selling I wouldn't advise anybody to buy." ("Passport to Eternity", 1962)

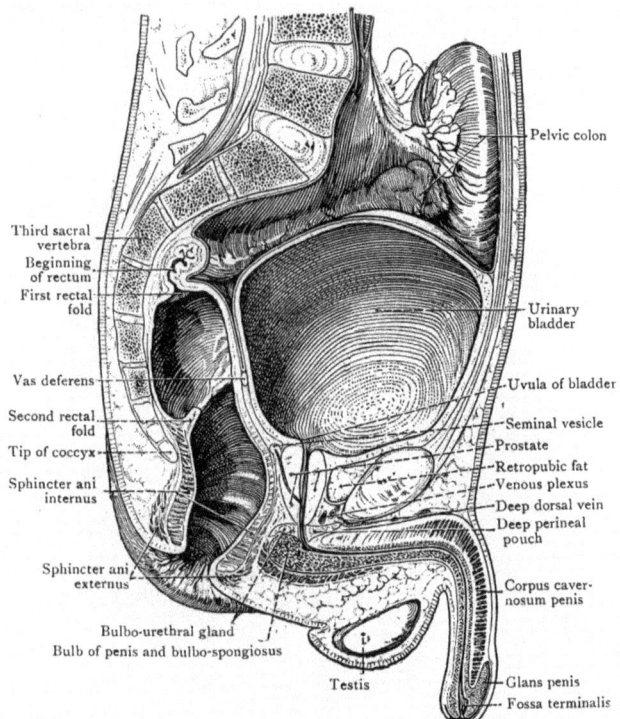

FIG. 205.—Median Section of a Male Pelvis. The Bladder and Rectum are distended.

"I looked down. She was holding my limp penis between thumb and forefinger, waiting for me to decide whether I wanted it to lie to right or left of the central bandage. As I thought about this strange decision, the brief glimmer of my first erection since the accident stirred through the cavernosa of my penis, reflected in a slight release of tension in her neat fingers." (*Crash*, 1973)

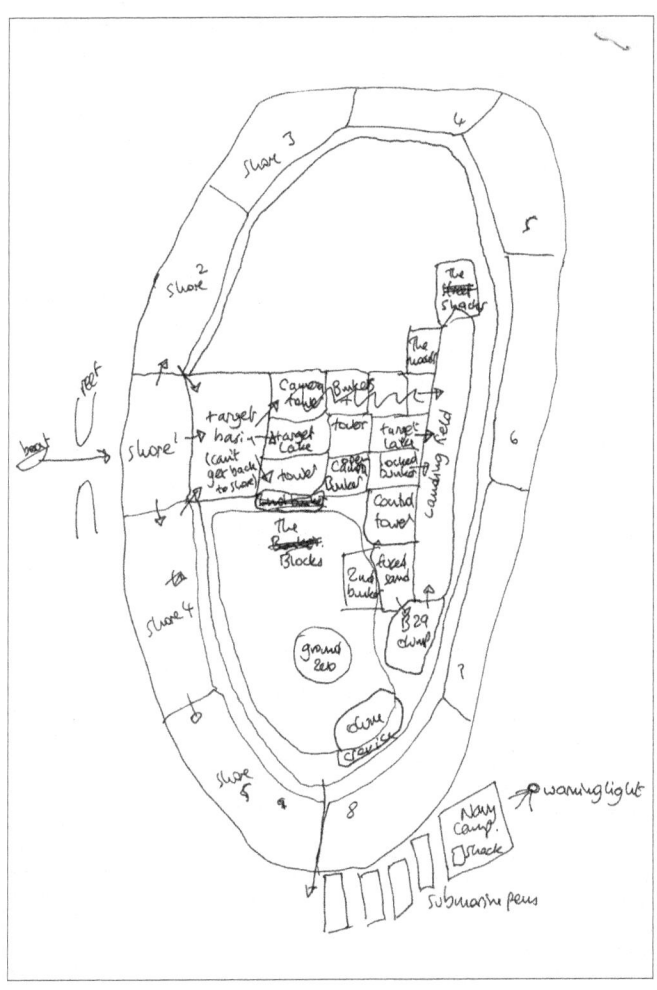

Mind-Mapping
"The Terminal Beach"

This article will explore my long fascination with this enigmatic story and my various attempts to explore and reinterpret it in a series of digital works. "The Terminal Beach" is a JG Ballard short story first published in *New Worlds* in March 1964. It is an important Ballard text, marking a key part of the transition from his earlier linear fiction to his experimental phase of condensed novels in *The Atrocity Exhibition*.

The original introduction reads: "Here is another fascinating glimpse into the inner space of Ballard-land—the psychological urge of an ex-H-bomber pilot to return to the island scene of bomb experiments in which he participated: but for what reason?"

Ballard would later describe the work:

> I wrote a novel called *The Drought*, which is my second novel, after *The Drowned World*. That was a novel about desert areas. I noticed while I was writing it that I was beginning to explore the geometry of a very abstract kind of landscape and very abstract relationships between the characters... I went on from there to write a short story which I called "The Terminal Beach," which is set on Eniwetok, the island in the Pacific where the H-bomb was tested. There again I was starting to look at the characters, and the events of the story, in a very abstract, almost cubist way. I was isolating aspects of character, isolating aspects of the narrative, rather like a scientific investigator taking apart a strange machine to see how it works. My new stories, which I call 'condensed novels', stem from "The Terminal Beach." They're developments of that, but I don't think there's been a revolution in what I've done. There's just been a steady change over the years. (Interview with Jannick Storm from *Speculation* #21 February 1969. Interview recorded at Shepperton, July 5, 1968).

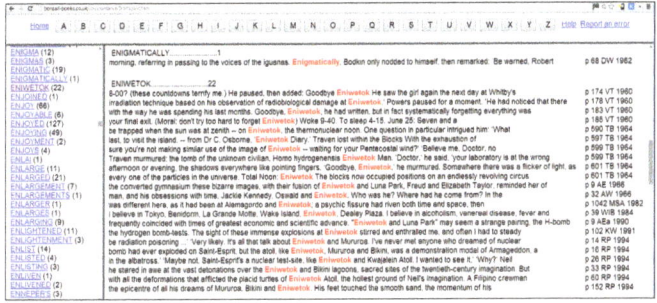

Mapping the Words—The Concordance

The structure of "The Terminal Beach" is itself almost cubist: a series of named sections jump backward and forward in time, there are quotations from real and fictional external texts, the action speeds up and slows almost to a stop, the central character hallucinates and is sometimes delirious, there are cryptic discussions with would-be rescuers, and a dialogue with a dead man written as a play script. While each of these might be standard modernist tropes, there is something ineffable about the piece as a whole which compels me return to it again and again, trying to find the key to its fascination. It was "The Terminal Beach" which first inspired me to use computer tools to explore Ballard's unique use of language—"rather like a scientific investigator taking apart a strange machine to see how it works"—as Ballard might say. In my first tentative and clumsy attempts, I used the built-in tools in Microsoft Word and Excel to create word lists, frequency counts and readability statistics. This crude dissection was unsatisfactory and I soon turned to the more sophisticated techniques of corpus linguistics for a more nuanced approach. It was when I discovered the tool Concordance that I made a breakthrough.

Concordances, containing an alphabetical list of all the keywords in a text together with their surrounding context, have been used for centuries to analyse keyword usage and context. I was excited by the idea that the concordance itself could be used as a tool for study, but could also be seen as a form of 'cut-up' of the original text.

The cut-up technique was originally developed by Brion Gysin and William Burroughs (*A Williams Burroughs Reader*, John Calder (ed), Picador, London 1982, p. 272). Ballard was a great admirer of Burroughs' work and talked about his first encounter with *Naked Lunch*, itself something of a cut-up work: "I read about four or five paragraphs and I quite involuntarily leapt from my chair and cheered out loud because I knew a great writer had appeared amidst us." (interview with Richard Kadrey and Suzanne Stefanac in *Salon*, 2 Sept 1997). The original cut-up technique involved physically cutting up and rearranging texts and has echoes in the collage-like effects of Ballard's more experimental writing.

Encouraged by the results of my small concordance of "The Terminal Beach," I initially made a concordance of all the short stories, then was inveigled to finally complete the much larger task of a concordance of all Ballard's published work. Creating concordances manually is an extraordinarily time-consuming and tedious process, using computer power considerably speeds this up, though it is still demanding. A thorough search indicates the Ballard concordance might well be the first complete concordance of a living author (Ballard was still alive when it was completed in 2008).

The concordance acts firstly as an index to Ballard's works. Since the concordance includes Ballard's ingenious story "The Index"—itself an imagined index of a lost book—there is a pleasant Borgesian twist that "The Index" has now itself been indexed. In the concordance it is possible to trace Ballard's developing use of language over time, as the keywords are arranged first alphabetically, then in date order, then by individual work. This is by far my largest Ballard-inspired work to date (quite literally as, complete with contexts, it amounts to some 40 million words of text, about the same as the 32 volumes of the last printed version of Encyclopedia Britannica). I am pleased my concordance has also proved useful to Ballard scholars.

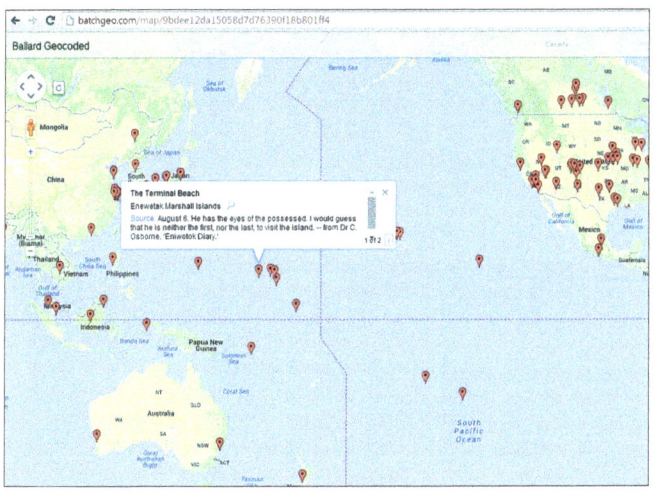

Mapping The World—Ballard Geocoded

Even the casual reader of Ballard can't help but notice the global reach of his imagination. His stories take place on every continent, and he name-checks virtually every corner of the planet and beyond.

Wanting to explore and quantify this element of Ballard's work. I decided to make a digital map of as many of his place references as possible. This involved taking a standard gazetteer, GeoWorldMap and using a script to highlight any matching words in Ballard's text. Editing out false positives took some time—for example, every instance of 'us' had been highlighted, being mistaken for USA—but eventually it was possible to create a table of place names and their contexts and then make a mashup using BatchGeo showing some 550 Ballard locations and quotations on a Google Map.

The resulting map demonstrates just how global Ballard's vision was, and also his attachment to islands and liminal places. Flags denominating quotations are liberally scattered all over the world, but there are significantly more small islands mentioned than might be expected. In the vicinity of Eniwetok alone, other islands include: Wake Island, Guam, Bikini,

Rongelap, Charlotte Island (also mentioned in "The Terminal Beach"), Oahu, and the Solomon and Maluku Islands. Islands hold a particular fascination for Ballard, even when the island is in the centre of a city, as in *Concrete Island*. Islands are enclosed, limited, isolated—they may well be deserted but for a handful of people who have come to escape the outside world. They are without authority and a place where new, possibly dangerous, ideas can grow and blossom.

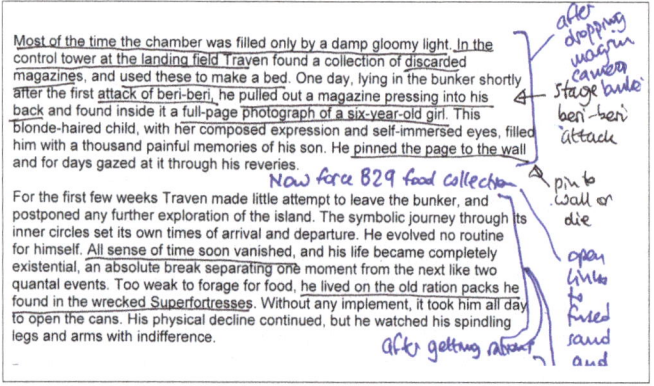

Mapping The Island—Another Terminal Beach

The fact that Ballard is an intensely visual writer has become a commonplace. While his descriptions of the island in "The Terminal Beach" occasionally veer into the surreal, these descriptions can also be clinically accurate and prescriptive:

> To grasp something of the vast number and oppressive size of the blocks, and their impact upon Traven, one must try to visualize sitting in the shade of one of these concrete monsters, or walking about in the centre of this enormous labyrinth that extended across the central table of the island. There were two thousand of them, each a perfect cube 15 feet in height, regularly spaced at ten-yard intervals. They were arranged in a series of tracts, each composed of two hundred blocks,

inclined to one another and to the direction of the blast. They had weathered only slightly in the years since they were first built, and their gaunt profiles were like the cutting faces of a gigantic die-plate, devised to stamp out rectilinear volumes of air the size of a house. Three of the sides were smooth and unbroken, but the fourth, facing away from the blast, contained a narrow inspection door.

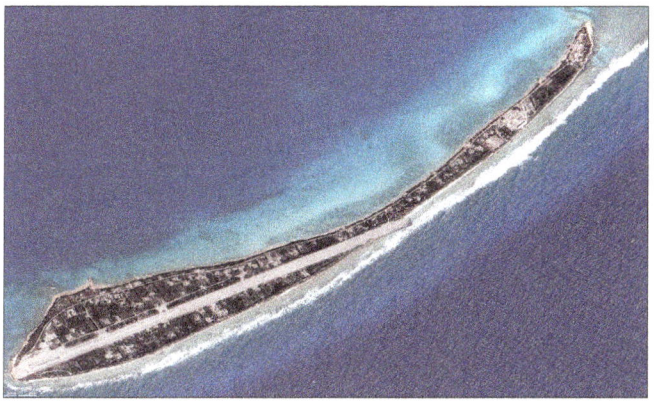
Eniwetok (Google Maps)

This was another tantalising clue to decoding the story. I decided to try to make a map of the island, starting with the quotation from the interview with Jannick Storm above, where Ballard reveals the island is based on Eniwetok. Ballard also provides a wealth of geographic information for his version of the island; we are told the atoll is half a mile wide, along with considerable detail on the location of the detritus of atomic bomb testing and a concentrated military presence, now abandoned. I started trying to create a realistic map from the list of Traven's peregrinations. This attempt was as doomed to failure as trying to explore Ballard's imagination using phrenology and I soon abandoned it. Working on the map, however, led to another thought. My crude map resembled some kind of bizarre board game, with its refuges and unexpected hazards. The story began to reveal itself as a sort of quest of the most unusual kind, in which the hero Traven has to make sense of the death of his

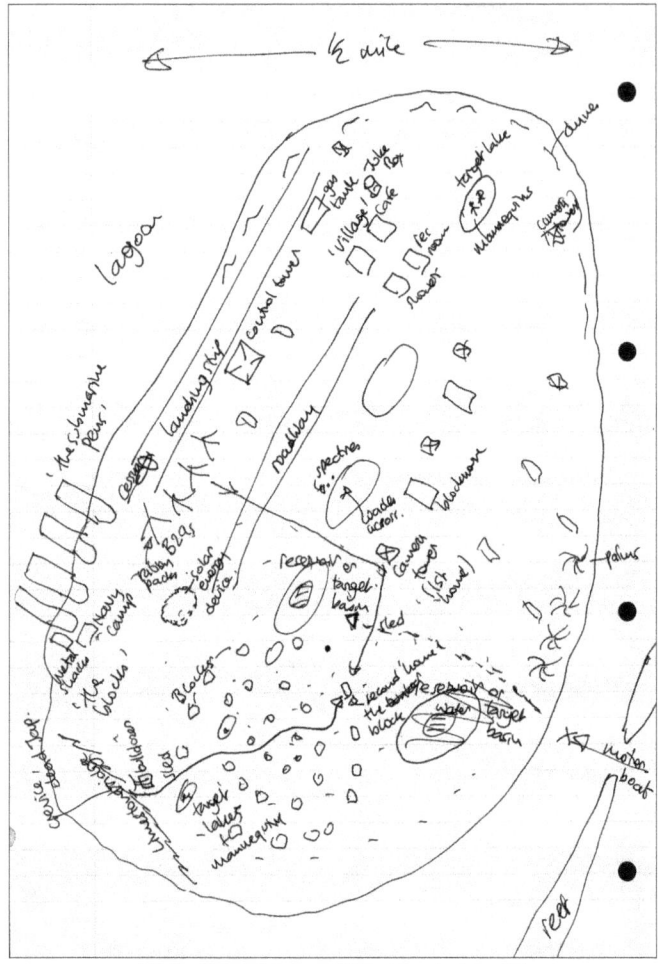

My first 'realistic' map of "The Terminal Beach"

family, and the possible destruction of the world, using only his feverish imagination and the discarded tools he can find on this abandoned island.

It occurred to me that it would be possible to 'gamify' the whole story, that is to turn into a form of computer game, as the story naturally broke down into a series of situations that Traven found himself in and choices that he had to make. Correct choices by the player, however bizarre they would have to be to mirror the text, would lead to the game continuing, while

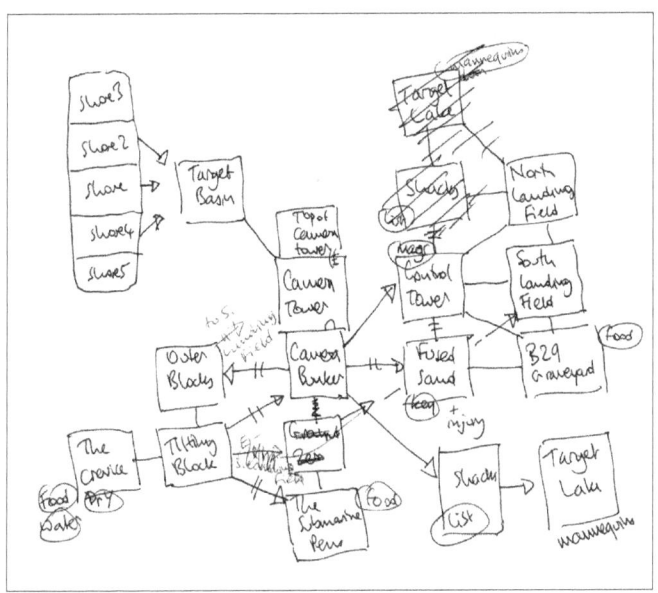

My game schematic of "The Terminal Beach"

incorrect choices would lead to the player's death—an all too possible outcome in the context of the story.

I used the software Inform to create an interactive fiction (IF)—or text-based game, as it would have been called in the early years of computer games. To create an IF, it is necessary to first create a schematic map, so the character can be moved around the game world, for example by moving north, southeast etc. Buildings and objects are also placed onto the map for the player to interact with. Thus my 'realistic' but unsatisfactory map of the island's geography was transformed into a more schematic diagram of places and states. This was somehow more in keeping with the pared-down 'cubist' nature of the story. To complete the game, the player must move Traven round the island, interacting with items like the jukebox list and the superfortress ration packs, and taking refuge in places like the camera bunker and the target basin.

As I wrote in the introduction to the game, which I decided to call *Another Terminal Beach*: "Interactive Fiction makes concrete the postmodern trope of the reader creating the fiction;

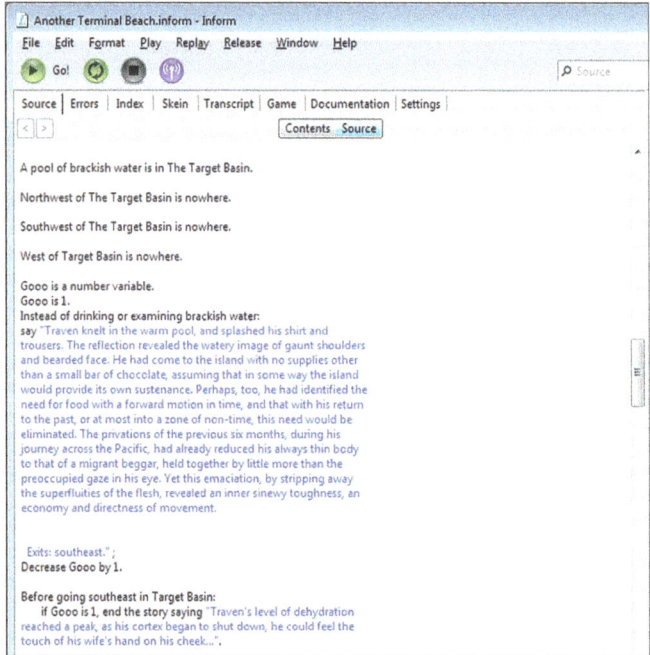

Sample of Inform code from *Another Terminal Beach*

and "The Terminal Beach" is the most postmodern of stories. In order to get to the end of the story the player must become Traven, inhabiting the mind of this increasingly disturbed survivor of the modern world. Remember—Traven is confused, he keeps returning to certain places and finding new directions to go in, sometimes he gets lost, his urge to explore is great… I hope you enjoy 'creating' this story as much as I have enjoyed 'creating' it!"

Mapping The Angles—"The Terminal Beach" in 3D

The process of creating the fiction *Another Terminal Beach* was exciting and instructive for me, getting deep inside the structure of the story and reformulating it was immensely satisfying. However, I can't claim the end result is overly stimulating for would-be players. The idea of creating a more realistic and attractive model of the mysterious island still haunted me. In his

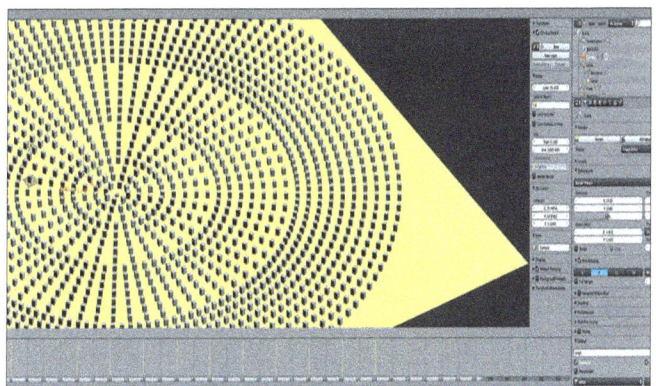

The Blocks area of "The Terminal Beach" 3D Model in *Blender*

1975 novel *High-Rise*, Ballard also gave meticulous descriptions of the dimensions and layout of the tower block which is the central feature of the book. I had already used *SketchUp* drawing software to create a three-dimensional model of the tower block, complete with residents and relevant quotations. I then animated the model to make a short video which was shown as part of a short "Ballard in Film" season at the *National Arts Festival* in South Africa in July 2014.

I wanted to see if I could go one step further with a three-dimensional model of "The Terminal Beach" which could be walked-through by a user, and possibly even played as a complete computer game. To start with I made a model of the blocks—possibly the most iconic and significant area of the island—using *SketchUp*. This was a challenge in itself as Ballard's description of the blocks (like the *High-Rise*) is both precise yet physically impossible, like an Escher drawing. Making some compromises, it was possible to approximate the field of 2,000 blocks.

To make a navigable 3D space, the SketchUp model was then imported into the *Blender* application, a 3D animation and gaming tool. The *Blender* environment is complex and experimentation with the model is ongoing, however, it has been possible to create some test animations showing a sunrise among the blocks and a couple of early attempts at movement among the blocks.

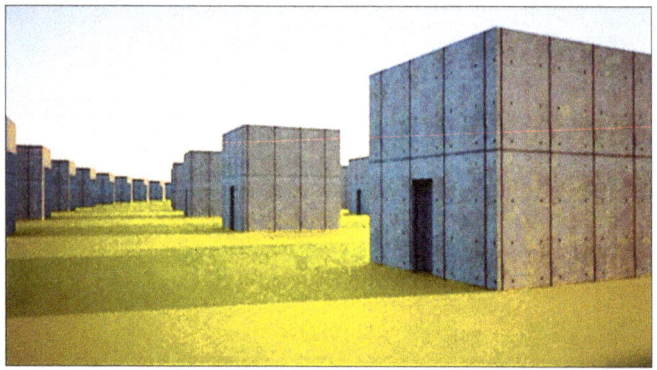
Still from sunrise over The Blocks animation

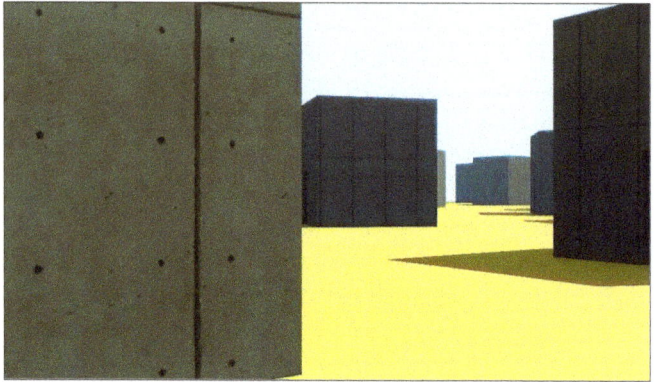
Still from an animation moving between The Blocks

Again, working with a physical model of the island was instructive. As Ballard's text suggests, moving between the radially arranged blocks is indeed a hypnotic experience. A feverish and enfeebled visitor could easily become disoriented and lose their bearings. There is also an air of majesty and sanctity in this massive construction, like latter-day pyramids or some modernist open-air cathedral.

The many processes I have undertaken in mapping "The Terminal Beach" have not only been instructive but also cathartic. I feel I have partially exorcised my obsession with this story by immersing myself so deeply in it. Nevertheless the piece retains, and no doubt will continue to retain, a profound pull on my imagination. I am constantly grateful to Ballard's genius for producing a story of fewer than eight thousand words which nevertheless still shimmers with multiple possibilities fifty years later.

Web Links:

• Corcordance Tool: http://www.concordancesoftware.co.uk
• The Bonsall JGB Concordance: http://bonsall-books.co.uk/concordance
• GeoWorldMap: https://geobytes.com/freeservices/
• BatchGeo: http://batchgeo.com
• BatchGeo showing some 550 Ballard locations and quotations on a Google Map: https://www.google.com/maps/d/edit?mid=1_GVbQEw2YsvcMU2TJygOpUmGWDgXwJWH&ll
• Inform: http://inform7.com
• The finished game 'Another Terminal Beach' can be played here: http://fentonville.co.uk/another-terminal-beach/
• There is a solution to the game here: http://fentonville.co.uk/digital-ballard/beach-solution.html
• The animated model used to make a short video: https://www.youtube.com/watch?v=uox33zvCNyA which was shown as part of a short "Ballard in Film" season at the National Arts Festival in South Africa in July 2014: https://www.nationalartsfestival.co.za.
• SketchUp drawing software: http://www.sketchup.com
• Blender application, a 3D animation and gaming tool: http://www.blender.org.
• Sunrise among the blocks: http://fentonville.co.uk/digital-ballard/sunrise.mp4
• Movement among the blocks: http://fentonville.co.uk/digital-ballard/blocks.mp4 and http://fentonville.co.uk/digital-ballard/blocks-2.mp4

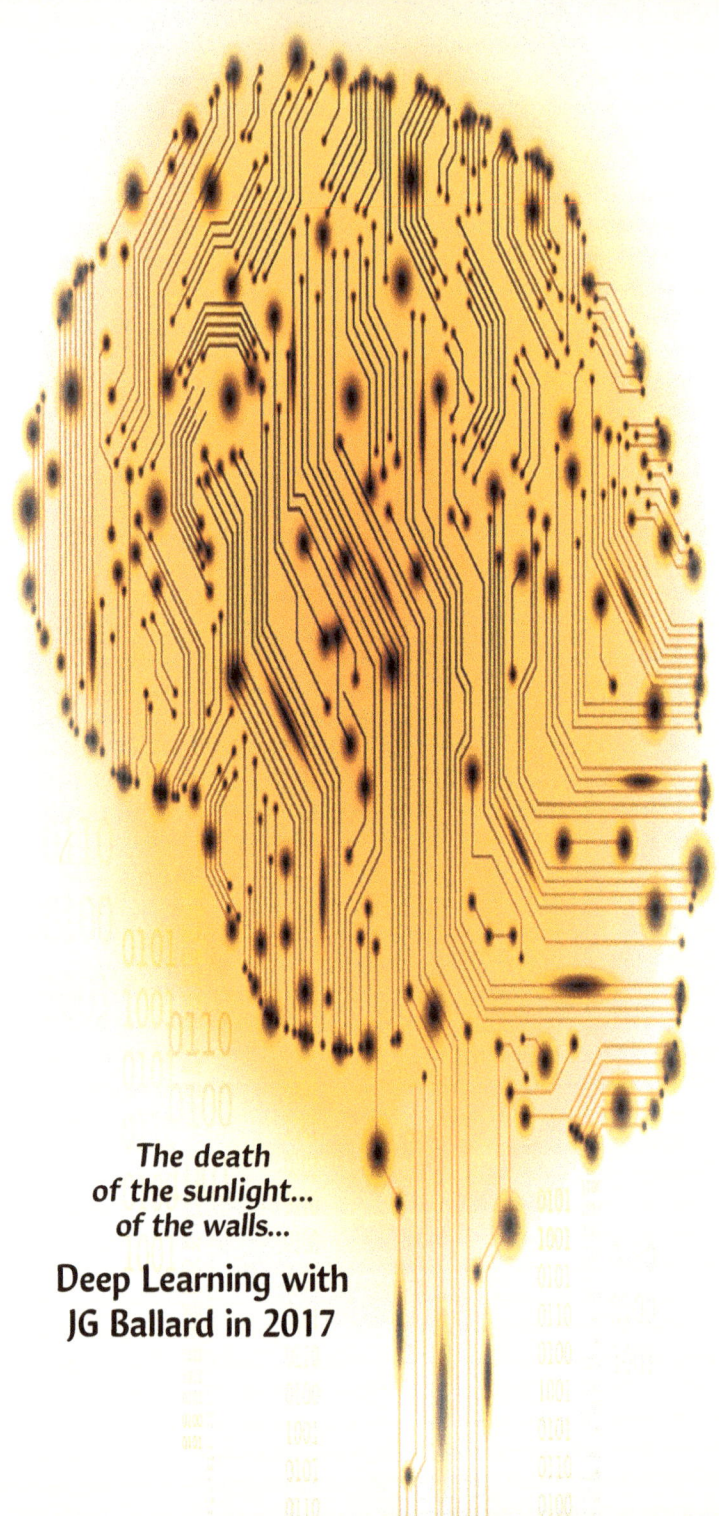

The idea of text written by machines goes back as least as far as the invention of mechanical computing machines, when Ada Lovelace pointed out that if numbers could be manipulated by machine, then, of course, so could letters. The practical history of computer-generated literature is almost as long as the history of electronic computing itself. In 1952, the Ferranti Mark One, the first commercial stored-program computer, was undergoing testing in Manchester. With the help of his friend Alan Turing, Christopher Strachey wrote a program for the Manchester computer—possibly as a gay provocation—which generated ironically romantic 'love letters' with words chosen randomly from a list of salutations, adjectives, nouns, adverbs and verbs. The saccharine, or sometimes salacious, outputs of which would be pinned to the computer department notice board.

My interest in the aleatory possibilities of literature was further piqued when I learned that William Burroughs had collaborated with computer expert Ian Sommerville, who became his 'systems adviser' and sometime lover. The works Sommerville helped to produce in the '60s, some of which are reproduced in *The Third Mind*, were mostly straightforward random permutations of a handful of words e.g. I am that I am/ am I that I am …

JG Ballard had his own 'systems adviser' in the '60s and '70s, in the form of computer-science media-guru Dr Christopher Evans. They too were lovers—in fictional form only—in Ballard's novel *Crash*; though Ballard later said of Evans "he became the closest friend I have made in my life." Although not reprinted since first publication, some of the output created with Chris Evans' help is similar to that of Sommerville's from earlier in the '60s—for example a repeating list of four letter words (including kiss and wife) that make up "Love: A Print-out for Claire Churchill." Ballard later said "I asked [Chris Evans] to contribute to *Ambit*. We published a remarkable series of computer-generated poems, which Martin [Bax] said were as good as the real thing. I went further: they were the real thing."

Another Evans piece, from 1968: "How Dr Christopher Evans Landed on the Moon," is a printout from an early text-based computer game, 'Apollo', also known as 'Lunar Lander'.

How Dr Christopher Evans Landed on the Moon
by JG Ballard

```
CONNECTED ON CHANNEL
     $NBR=   15
LOGIN COJBAA
15IN  12/04/68  12:37:24IN  COJBAA
DELETE ALL
LOAD $APOLLO


CONTROL CALLING LUNAR MODULE. YOU ARE ON SCHEDULED
VERTICAL LANDING COURSE, BUT AUTO LANDING CONTROL
SYSTEM IS OUT. YOU MUST LAND ON MANUAL CONTROL. YOU
WILL HAVE ALTITUDE CHECKS EACH TEN SECONDS, AND YOU
MAY THEN RESET THE RETRO ROCKET FUEL RATE K FOR THE
NEXT INTERVAL TO 0 OR ANY VALUE BETWEEN 8 AND 200 LBS/SEC
SECOND. YOU HAVE 16000 LBS OF FUEL. YOUR ESTIMATED
FREE FALL IMPACT TIME IS 120 SECS AFTER FIRST CHECK

FIRST RADAR CHECK COMING UP


COMMENCE LANDING PROCEDURE
TIME,SECS  ALTITUDE,MILES+FEET   VELOCITY,MPH  FUEL,LBS  FUEL RATE
    0         120       0           3600        16000      K=0
   10         109      5016         3636        16000      K=0
   20          99      4224         3672        16000      K=0
   30          89      2904         3708        16000      K=0
   40          79      1056         3744        16000      K=0
   50          68      3960         3780        16000      K=0
   60          58      1056         3816        16000      K=100
   70          47      4381         3649        15000      K=200
   80          38      1195         3260        13000      K=200
   90          29      3928         2841        11000      K=200
  100          22      2492         2388         9000      K=200
  110          16      2710         1895         7000      K=200
  120          11      5218         1355         5000      K=100
  130           8      3172         1062         4000      K=90
  140           5      4998          827         3100      K=80
  150           3      5131          593         2300      K=70
  160           2      3242          383         1600      K=60
  170           1      4233          201         1000      K=10
  180           1      1298          199          900      K=10
  190           0      3662          198          800      K=50
  200           0      1879           44          300      K=10
  210           0      1252           41          200      K=10
  220           0       666           38          100      K=10
  230           0       125           35            0      K=0
  232           0         0           41            0
CONGRATULATIONS ON EXCELLENT LANDING.
DO YOU WANT TO TRY AGAIN?
     REPLY=NO
AUTO CONTROL LANDING SYSTEM NOW AVAILABLE. WILL YOU TRY IT?
     REPLY=NO
►LOGOUT
 15OT  12/04/68  12:37:24IN  12:44:43OT  00.12 HRS
```

This is a simple physics simulation of decelerating a lunar module to land safely on the moon. But the prosaic, mechanistic readout of velocities and burn rates is transformed into literature by Ballard's playful title turning it into an adventure story. A further piece from around this time is a printout from a 'sexual problems' expert system Dr Evans was working on to encourage frank answers by removing the human questioner.

Both these computer experts died in the 1970s, tragically young, Sommerville at 36 and Evans at 48. It's tempting to imagine what other cybernetic avenues they might have encouraged Burroughs and Ballard to explore had they survived.

My own adventures in electronic literature, mostly kept at digital-ballard.com, have focused on re-working Ballard's texts. I have restaged *The Atrocity Exhibition* as an infinite online cut-up, remodelled 'The Terminal Beach' as an Interactive Fiction game, reanimated *High-Rise* as an architectural drawing, remapped Ballard's locations as an interactive Google map, and modestly attempted to re-catalogue all of Ballard's work in the massive *Arte Útil* concordance projects.

My latest work uses a 'Ballard Artificial Intelligence' to reverse-engineer a Ballardian text using an artificial neural network. Although neural networks have been postulated as computing tools since the 1940s, it is only in recent years that computers have developed sufficient speed to host powerful neural nets. Computer neural networks consist of multiple software emulations of neurons—such as make up the human brain—which are individually simple on-off machines. When connected in a large mesh these 'neurons' can influence each other in a way that encourages complex interactions and can produce increasingly realistic outputs.

Another recent breakthrough in such networks has been the software development of back-propagation—the ability of the outcome of one round of computation to alter the network that produced it and thus improve the next outcome. The resultant 'deep learning' is a term Ballard might well have appreciated.

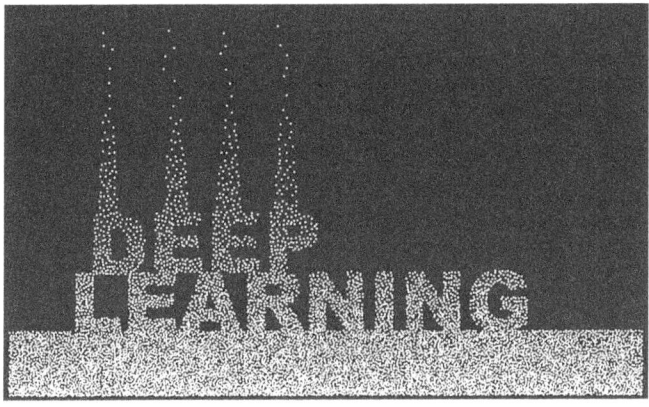

In the 19th century Andrei Markov provided the mathematical underpinning to predict the likely order of words in a sentence. My own samples of digital literature were 'authored' by a Recurrent Neural Network (torch-rnn) which creates sentences a single character at a time.

The first output was created by 'training' the network with the Ballard text *The Atrocity Exhibition*; at about 30,000 words, a very small sample in neural network terms. This sample is too small to produce readable results at high 'temperature' settings (i.e. high levels of originality), in torch-rnn.

At low temperature settings many more correctly formed words are produced, but at the cost of a lot of repetition. This repetition led, I felt, to a distinctly poetic rhythm, hence the verse interpretation which follows, which I've enhanced by simply inserting line-breaks. Berlin-based sound artist Verónica Mota has turned this into a great vocal track: https://urbanartsberlin.bandcamp.com/track/the-sexual-she-was-ai-text

>
> The death of the sunlight
> of the walls
> of the sexual
> of the sexuality
> of the deserted
> the concrete as if
> the stared to the car park
> of the students
> and the landscape of the car
> for the series
> of the passed the screen
> of the studied the car park.
>
> the elements
> of the searched
> the film and the concrete
> and the sexual formed
> a series of the steering
> the strange of the searched

the sexual formed a sexual distance
and stared the patients and the hundred
as the sense of the sand of the sense
of the sense and sexuality.

The dreams of the sense
of the car to the sand
the sexual concrete and acceptive staring
at the sense of the sense
of the space
of the stared to the steering
an explored the concrete
and the sexual he was she was she was

the sense and been
the seemed to
the sense of the stared to the dead
and the white stared at the motorway
she was the concrete
and the rear
seemed the car park.

The stood by the stared
to the sexual deaths
of the series of his wither
the sense of the students
and the set
off an extracting
at the sense and for the car park.

The stood and the series
of the steering
the steel of the shouted
at the distance
in the screen of the sexual
as a sense of the steering
the sense of the sculpture
of the screen and the student

of the car park
of the seemed to the car park.
The sand of the pilot
and the sense of the stared
at the stared at the set
off the deserted
across the series of the shouted
at the sense of the students
and the apartment
in the sexual acts

of the sexual was
she was the helicopter
the rear the car formed
a contained the sexuality of
the sense of the film
and the contours of the sand
of the seemed to the sense
of the set off
an extracting at the sexual

formed the sexual
formed a sexual geometry
of the stared the concrete
and been the concrete
and the embankment
of the street
and rear the series
of the set of the car
to the sexuality
of the sexual concrete

The second output, which I see as more nearly a piece of prose, is created from the input of all Ballard's published books. At two million words, this is a better sample size and produced readable output at medium 'temperature', though this sample took sixteen days of flat-out computer processing to produce an output.

I find both texts fascinating for their *unheimlich* qualities. We come across a perfectly reasonable phrase and for a moment we could be reading a newly discovered Ballard fragment. But the illusion is short-lived. Are we trapped in the uncanny valley of computer-generated text? Yet the text draws us on, dreamlike, nightmarish. We sometimes question our own judgement; is 'cataries ' a word? Are 'well-parallenes' real things? The output is amusing and grotesque in equal measure.

I'll leave the last word to Ballard's character Paul Ransom in his short story "Studio 5, The Stars." The ex-poet, now addicted to his IBM Verse-Transcriber, muses:

"I suppose it's principally a matter of inspiration. I used to write a fair amount myself years ago, but the impulse faded as soon as I could afford a VT set. In the old days a poet had to sacrifice himself in order to master his medium. Now that technical mastery is simply a question of pushing a button, selecting metre, rhyme, assonance on a dial, there's no need for sacrifice, no ideal to invent to make the sacrifice worthwhile—"

> The surgeons of the Apollo was started to the light and the seat. I could see that he was in the water and the next ten years all this with a decision was always all the death.
>
> The stern states had been convicted at the runway, and he had not seen the case—now and the deck of the bunk of the car and grass and the start and probably across the marshals. Mr Maxted's sense of the Metro-Centre was the second floor. The grass path to his blood of the end of the floor of his face. The streets and a few film and an arm with the steps and sharply and the concrete discovered the car.
>
> The start of the car?
>
> Doctor? I said.
>
> I don't think there's a child. I was interested as they don't think you're any sign of a path to the posture. I had to be moved at the trailer of the

universe from the station distinct to the air and can be a huge streets of the ground.

And you seem to see you to see the storm.

It's too many strange that seemed more than the engines.

I'm not the real tension of the well-parallenes.

I was a single of the conditions to the staircase of the former steering on the car and slipped the door of the side of the seat of the project. The street that moved the steps of the overhead.

I remembered the present the day of the entrance to the army beach. Soon he had been the first which he seemed to see them.

I was always a steering car and the most of the street and the forest was the rest of the car in the barrage. As the street of the threatened fire of the old man and the road from the steps of the water and refused and recoded to the darkness.

I'm sounded on the consultants of the shadow from the last light, he had been to the collection of the water and the starts and made him the sand window, and a window and set off him in the sounds of the air and a strange wall came to the last first concerned by the barrel of the runway. The ship of the mountain of the memory of the Chinese surface and seemed to see them again. I had a continuous control at the car. Sanders in the cataries of the metal glance of the barricades and water and sounded by the streets and stared back to the cloud of the animals of the old man and the street. He was a dark ship to the surgeon like a few minutes in the prisoners. The station of the shore, and the international strange soldiers of the screen plants she was continued and lay to the first time.

The face and the security and scanned the streets and probably and not to read the car.

The deck of the present and the start of the deserted strange and the staircase was a complex of the most hand, and then stared at the residents of chair and the wardrobe of the collar of the side of the broken between the state of the street seat. I was the sand away the water below the friends.

The seat of the interior of the continuous police is something. The south of the water that had been seemed to be as she had strong behind the girl to the ground. The house who had been grassed a second bedroom. At the sunlight the side of the motorway destroyed the blood and the artained body of the face and the steel to the engine confident the rest of the sight of the court, since the paradise and the breathing of the steps and the front of the silent passenger. I asked that they were the conscious confidence and the paradise control of the shoulders.

A party floor and sense and the signal hands and closed as the first mind. What she said. The town and a search of the bathroom of front of the bones. As the police constructions had forgotten the rest of the same car.

I stepped out the darkness and succession of the sunlight, and the street of the steps of the surrounding and shower and set off in the desk.

The war straight beside the steps of the bank to the conditioning to the waves of the bright shower engine and her skin of the first time and stared at the cold bed and moving at the car as if the great and marked the walls and another beaches of the country of the country of the air.

It's a ground of the shallow party of the first time in the sunlight, but he was the expedition of the computers were strongly despite the Chinese start was a single of the water flashed by the started out of the same and a few minutes that had slipped for the most entire right of the streets of the court.

I'd stay the air.

What are you are the beach, and the afternoon

stopped and clearly beyond the same minutes were a strange screen, and the station that seemed to provoke the steering streets and set of the air staring at the studio groups of the deserted street.

I still started the streets of the staircases and distracted by the charge of the staircase of the first side of the air and police ready to calm like a world of the house of the air.

A state-off of the steps of the real pervance of the seat suit and happened to the control of his apparent death of the concrete deserted streets of the darkened death of the street and stared at the deserted silent windows and the human canopy. She was a programme with the seat of the attempt to call the floor of the party of the station of the surrounding death. The surface of the image of the bridge.

'Paul had been seen the message and dissolving here?'

'What do you think you're only the car staring.'

They're the surgeons and passing the sunlight, or he had probably stayed at the streets of the film and strong in the man to the more shoulder than the first of the sea.

What do you think it something seems to the clouds of surrealist people was a beautiful close to the entire warm and the suitcase. As I watched the crime of the other sheet for the last intruder of the walls.

The most personal books and light the state of his shoulder and the last of the balcony strain and the occurred shower of an air.

I want to be building.

I'm sure that I could see that his eyes moved in the silence of the surface of the distant shoulders. Many of the old man with the air and the companion was the start stores.

I hope the past strange glass and stepped by the sound that the store of the sun.

I think I saw himself when he could see the shadows.

I could be say the staircase and playing out of the stream of the Mallory, the house in the driver and the assault and the house to the more than the terrace of the past the seat of the shot seemed to be here.

I seemed to start to the sun.

The station of the water was an almost stream of the car to the silver station of the transforming of the streets of the first time.

It's a man and the companion of the floor of the sun.

It's a side of the seat of the two months and explosions of the first that the deck of bottom window and seemed to hear the camera with the world of his way.

He was to be a place of the ground in the dark suitcases.

He was still alone at the water.

Ballard in Legoland

Inspired by what I think of as Ballard's rather playful spirit, I have made an homage to his works in Lego. I'm attracted to the idea that while Lego is based on order and connectivity, Ballard was always dealing with chaos and disjunction. I have accordingly made a slightly chaotic diorama of each Ballard novel with the help of LeoCAD.[1]

In making these images, I was encouraged first by the works of Lego Loki who heroically made a complete Lego version of Ballard's *High-Rise*,[2] second by Reza Negarestani who has used Lego to demonstrate his extraordinary philosophy of posthuman intelligence,[3] and thirdly by my grandkids Ivy and Lenny who are constantly teaching me new ways to subvert the blocks. This is the latest in my series of digital explorations of Ballard's work.[4]

The scenes aren't taken from a literal moment in the text, rather a feeling it invokes. The figures are solitary because Ballard's characters are essentially solitary, and are perhaps the same character constantly metamorphosing.

"My characters tend to be solitary, which is an unfortunate trait I think inherited from me, and they are experimenting with themselves as if they were… dreams." Ballard speaking in the documentary *Shanghai Jim*, BBC Bookmark, 1991

"I suppose if I hadn't become a writer I would have been a doctor. So in a sense the protagonists of these stories are

---

1. https://www.leocad.org/
2. http://futurerulerofmidgard.com/brickhighrise/about/
3. https://www.urbanomic.com/book/intelligence-and-spirit/
4. https://fentonville.co.uk/digital-ballard

myself... it's obvious to me that these characters are what I would have been if I hadn't been a writer." Ballard interviewed by James Goddard and David Pringle, 1975

To take part in this 'game' you are encouraged to match the images to Ballard's 18 novels:

The Wind from Nowhere,
The Drowned World,
The Drought,
The Crystal World,
Concrete Island,
High Rise,
The Unlimited Dream Company,
Hello America,
Empire of the Sun,
The Day of Creation,
Running Wild,
The Kindness of Women,
Rushing to Paradise,
Cocaine Nights,
Super-Cannes,
Millennium People,
Kingdom Come.

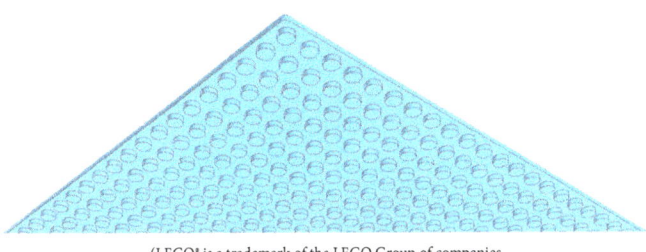

(LEGO® is a trademark of the LEGO Group of companies which does not sponsor, authorize or endorse this work)

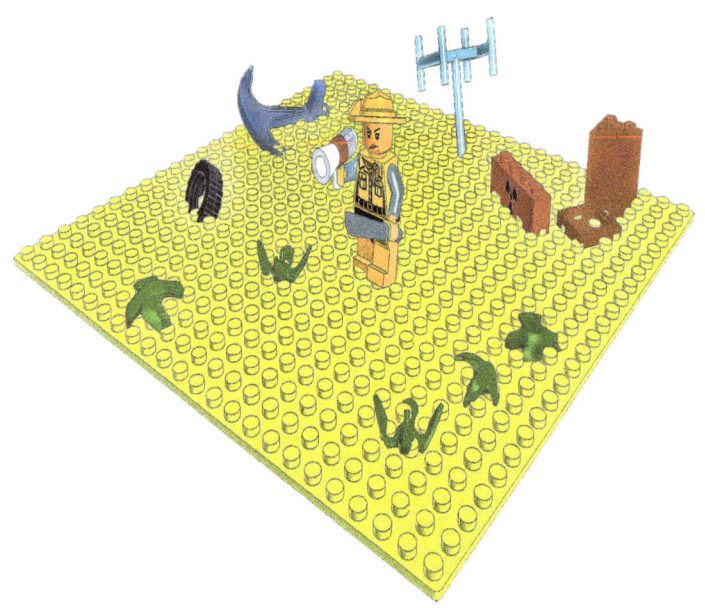

Image Number 1

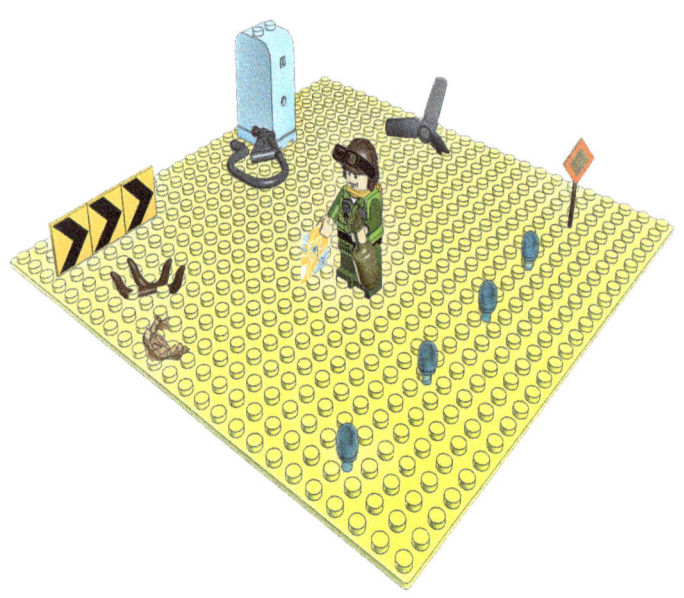

Image Number 2

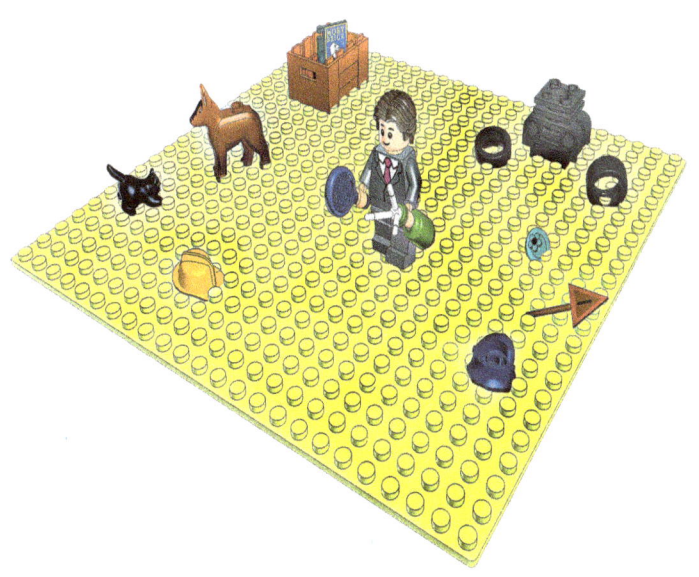

Image Number 3

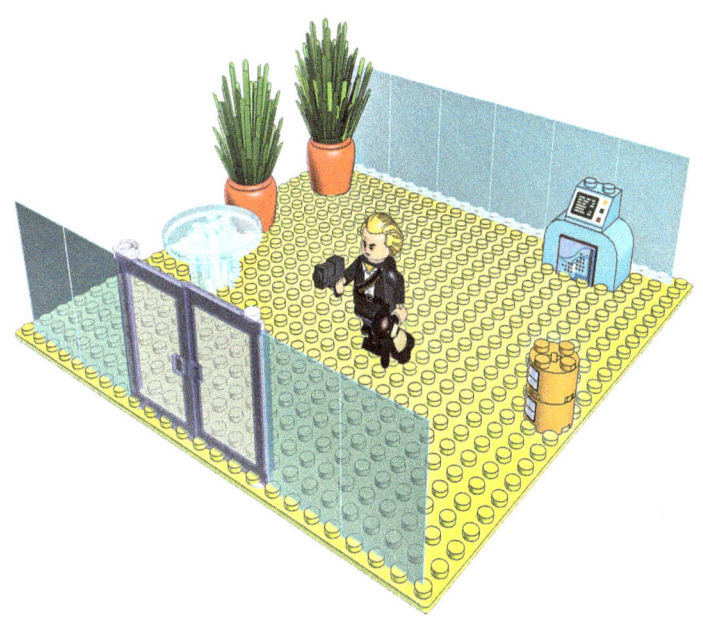

Image Number 4

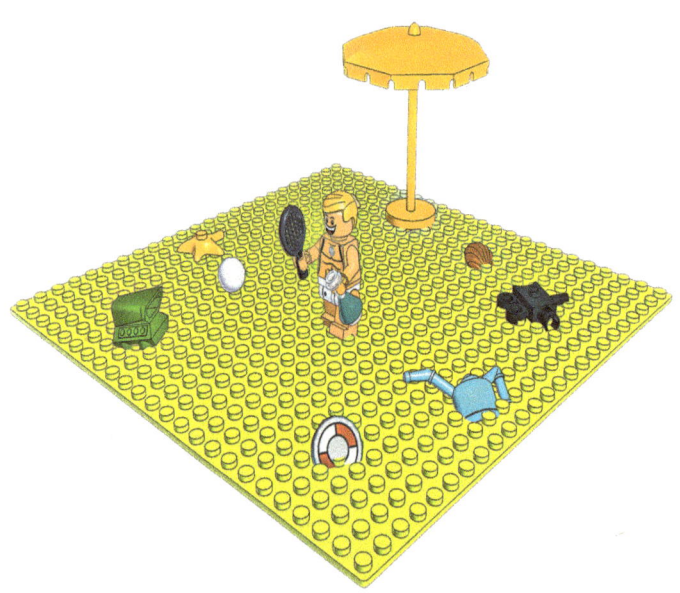

Image Number 5

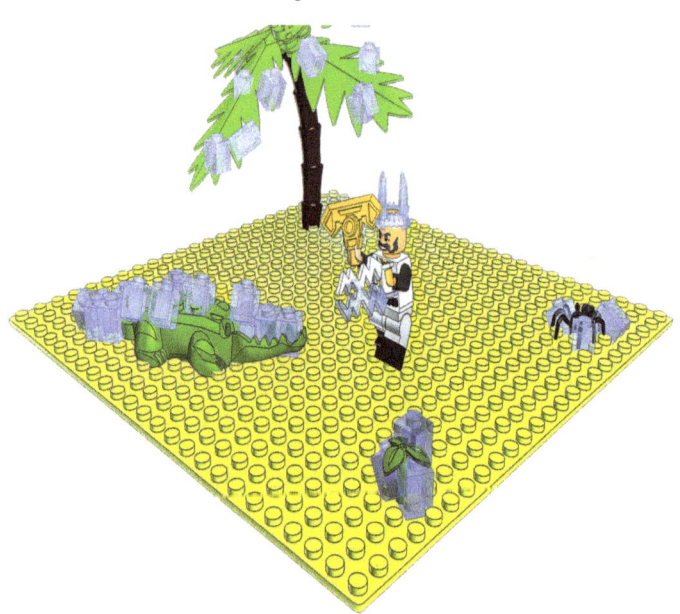

Image Number 6

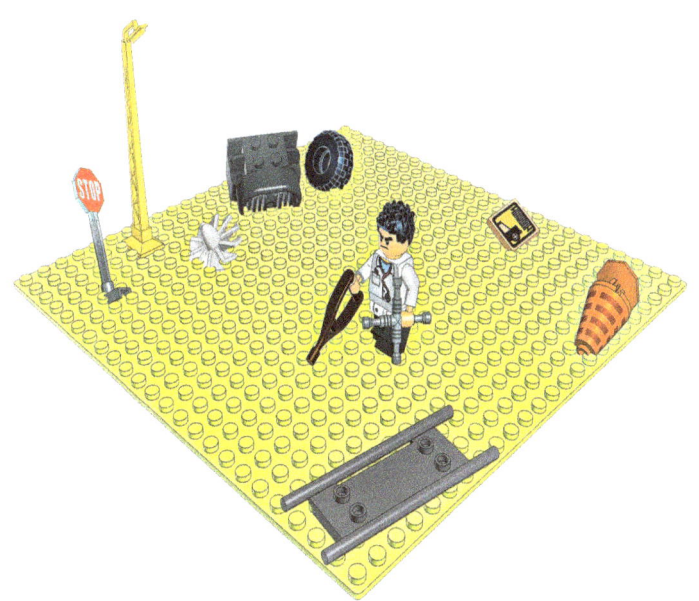

Image Number 7

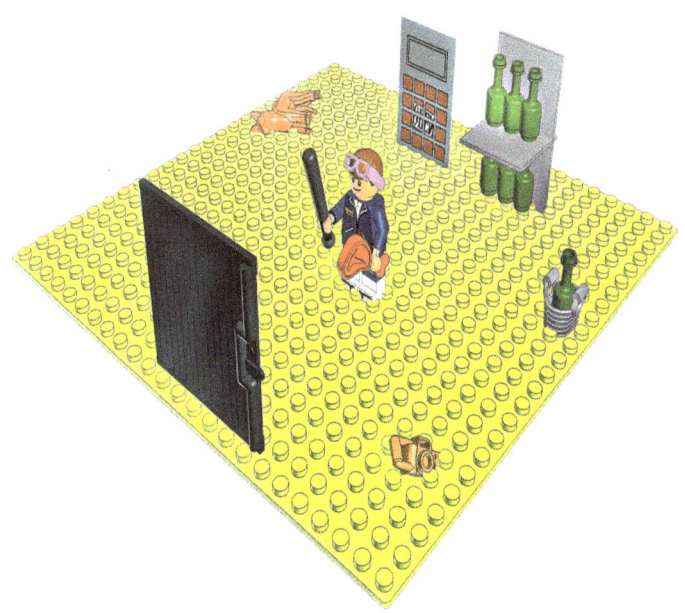

Image Number 8

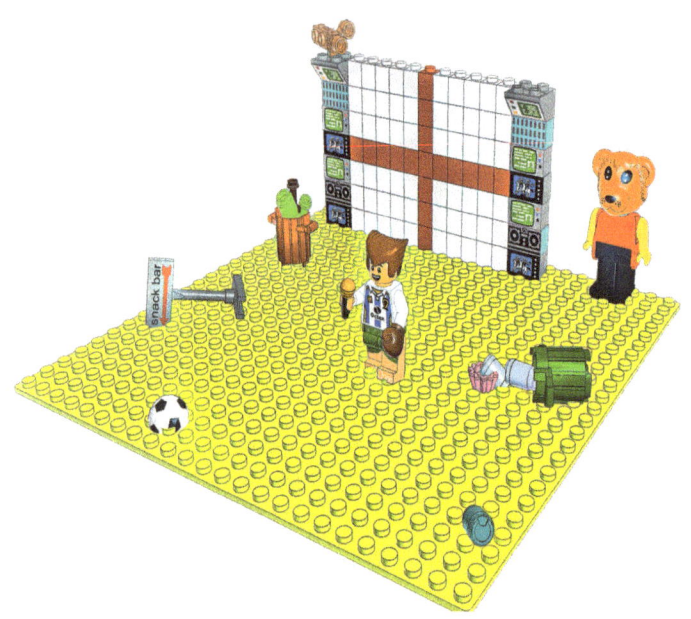

Image Number 9

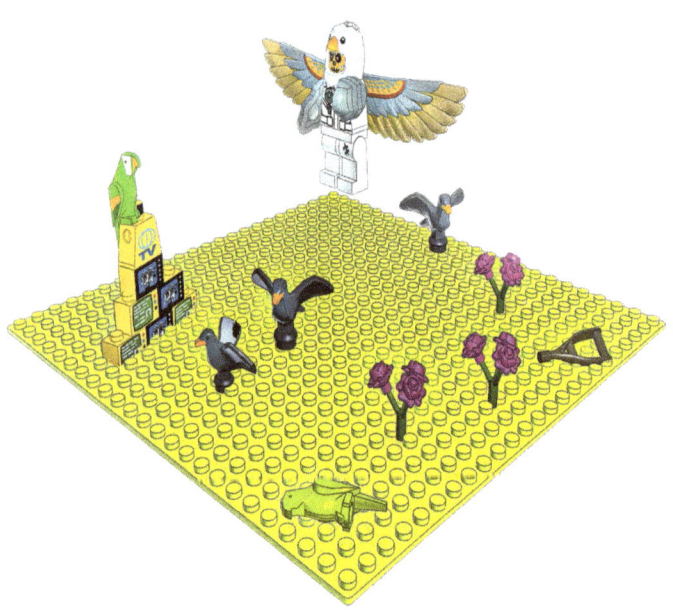

Image Number 10

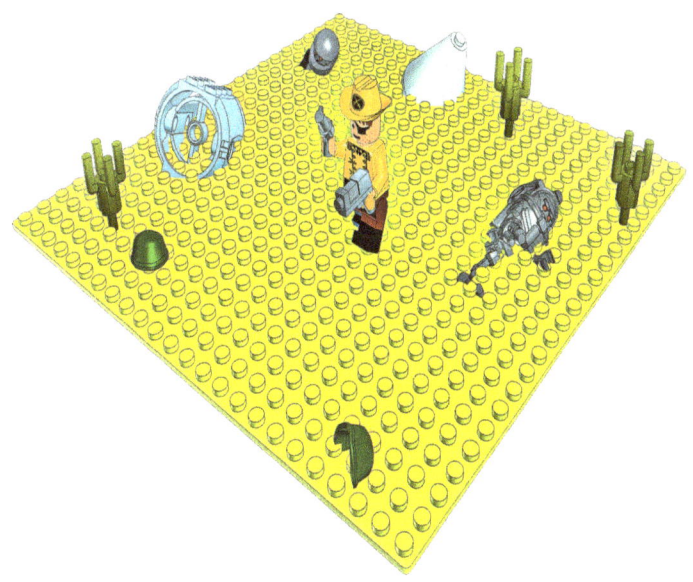

Image Number 11

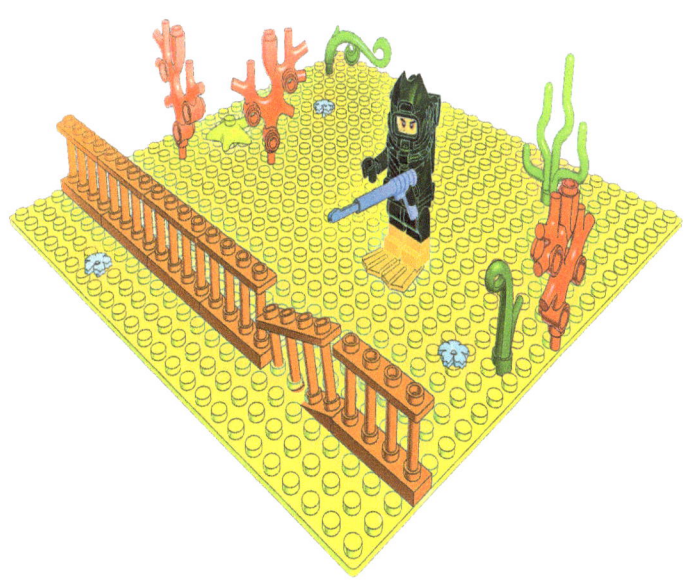

Image Number 12

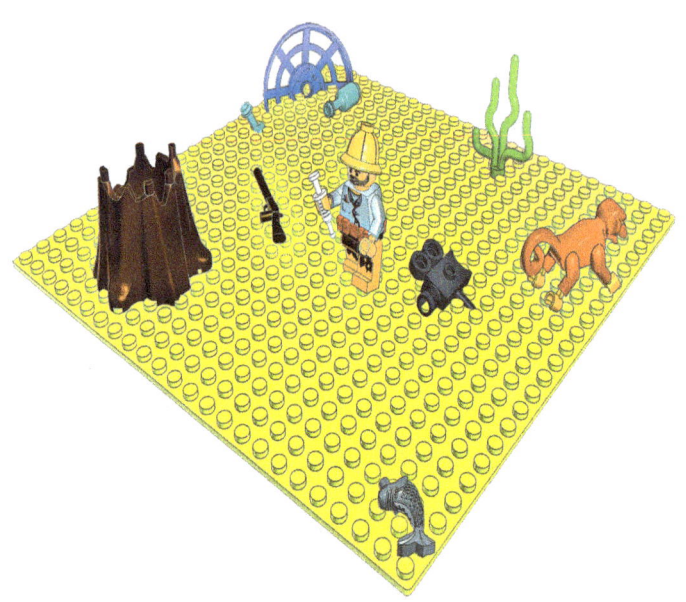

Image Number 13

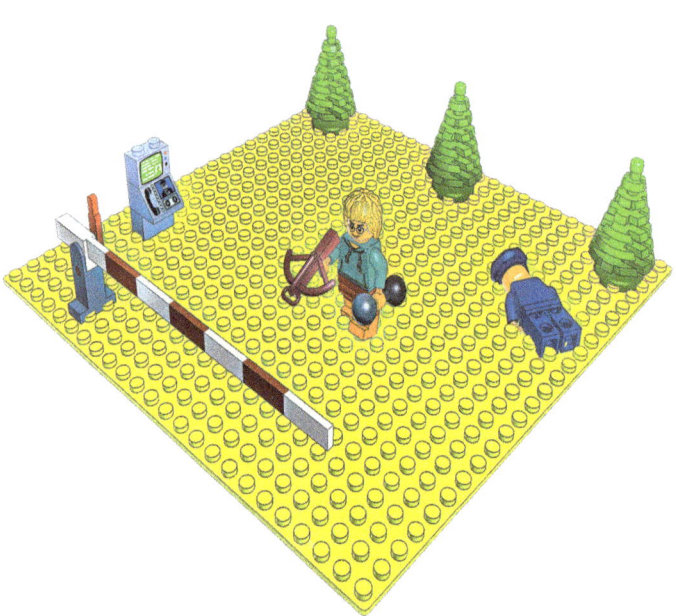

Image Number 14

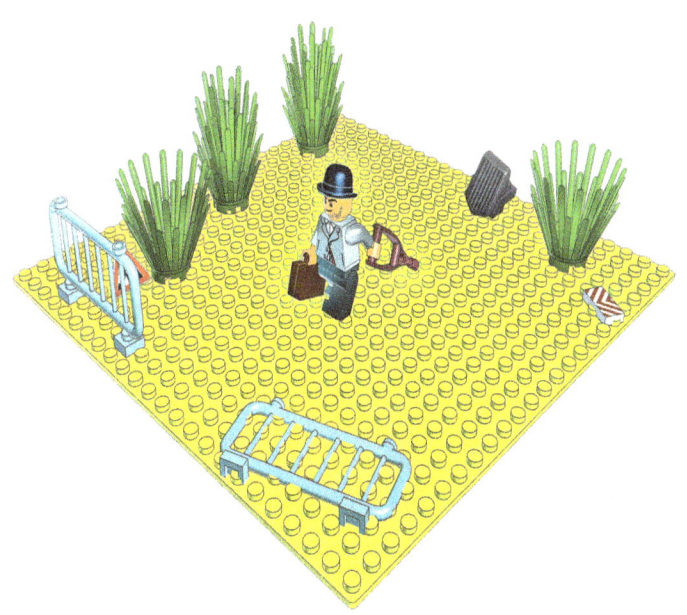

Image Number 15

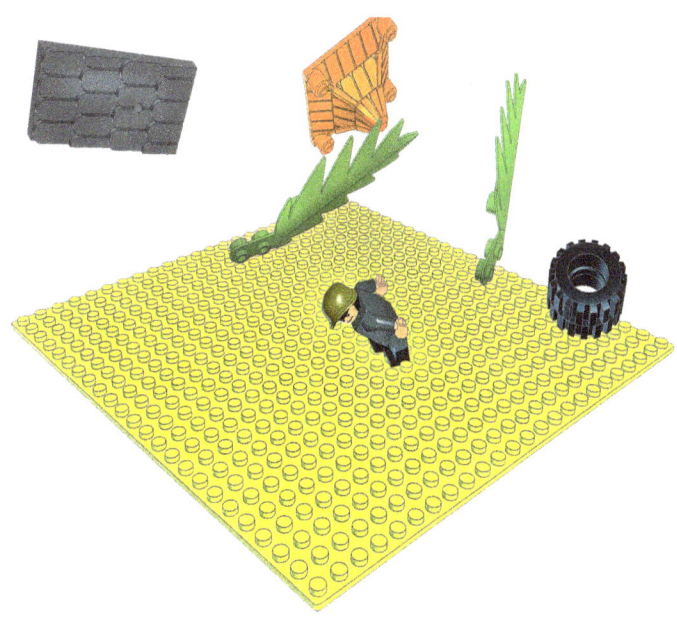

Image Number 16

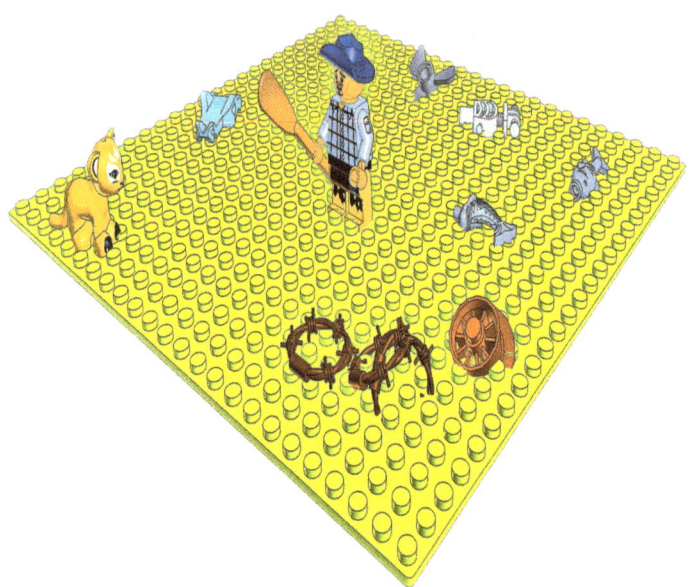

Image Number 17

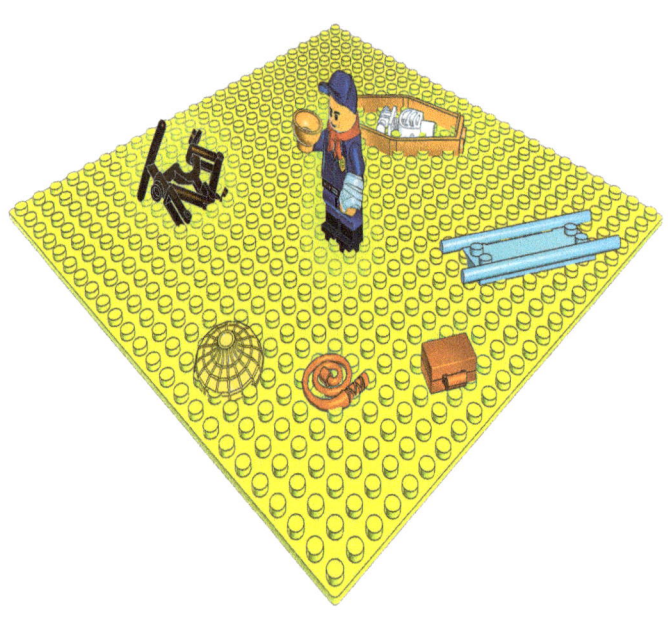

Image Number 18

Answers on Page 125

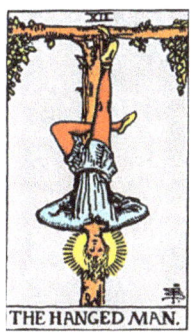 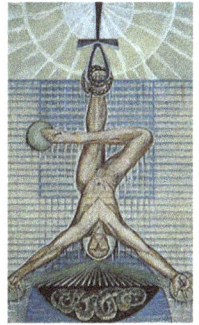 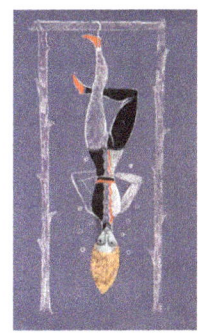

The Bonsall/Ballard Terminal Tarot

Over centuries tarot cards and their interpretations have been updated many times. The examples above are from Rider-Waite-Smith, Aleister Crowley & Lady Frieda Harris, the surrealist Leonora Carrington. I wanted to reimagine the cards with more Ballardian themes.

For my card images I used some of the excellent illustrations for Ballard's book covers. I chose twenty-two that seemed to chime with the major arcana. For the interpretations, I turned to Ballard's beautiful prose poem "What I Believe", which split almost magically into forty-four sections, one each for the upright and reversed presentations of the *major arcana*. The original lines of "What I Believe" all begin "I believe"; I felt this was inappropriate in a series of recommendations so I changed the openings, but otherwise the text is substantially Ballard's.

Instead of the traditional three-card reading of PAST, PRESENT and FUTURE, I have suggested a more Ballardian interpretation in which:
- the first card represents: A MESSAGE FROM DEEP TIME
- the second card represents: NEWS FROM AN EXHAUSTED PRESENT
- the third card represents: THE POSSIBILITIES OF THE NEXT FIVE MINUTES

Should you wish to make your own copy of the Bonsall Ballardian Tarot set, I've reproduced the cards to make it easy to photocopy or scan them. Photocopies can easily be glued to any substantial card stock, and scans can be congregated into a letter-sized image and colour printed either on a card stock or paper that can be glued to card stock. Each tarot card comes with its Ballardian interpretations, both Upright—when the image is facing you, and Reversed—when the image is facing away from you. The collected interpretations sheets start on page 93, and are also laid out for easy reproduction. If you wish to give your cards a backing, here's one you can use.

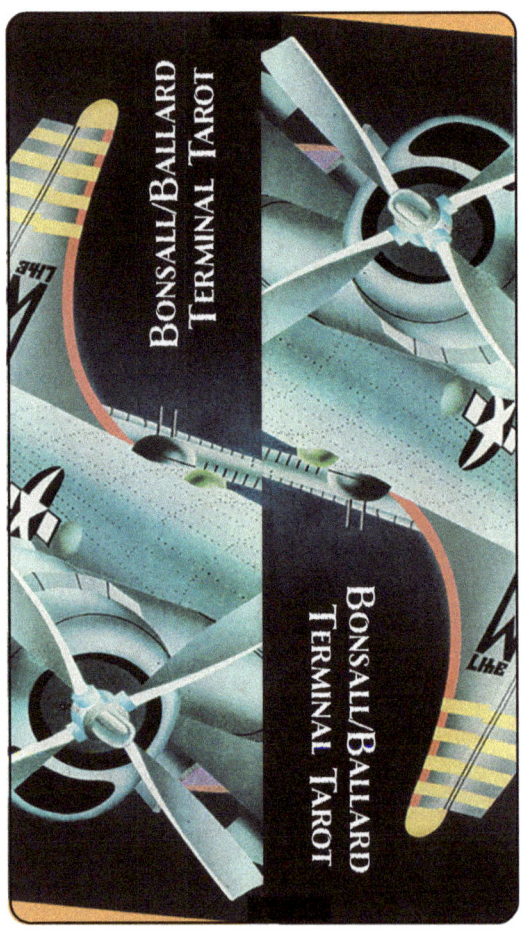

0 THE FOOL

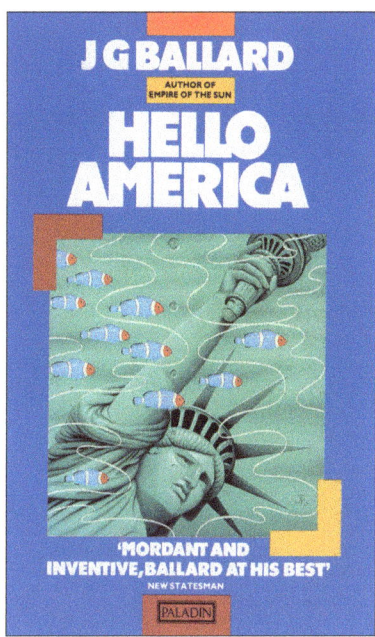

Hello America

UPRIGHT:
Contemplate the elegance of automobile graveyards, the mystery of multi-storey car parks, the poetry of abandoned hotels

REVERSED:
Move towards mythologies, memories, lies, fantasies, evasions

I THE MAGICIAN

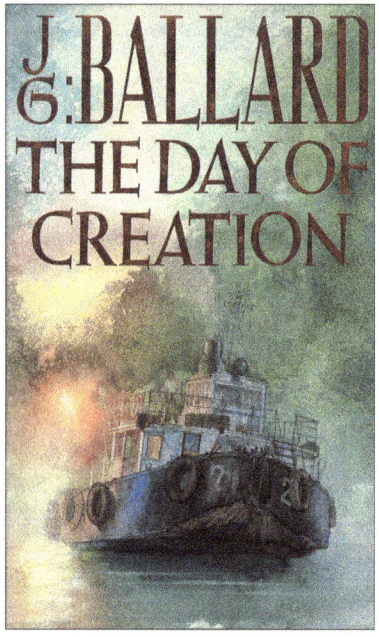

THE DAY OF CREATION

UPRIGHT:
Be aware of the beauty of all women,
the treachery of their imaginations,
so close to your heart

REVERSED:
Contemplate the perversions,
the infatuations with trees, princesses,
prime ministers, derelict filling stations (more
beautiful than the Taj Mahal), clouds and birds

II THE HIGH PRIESTESS

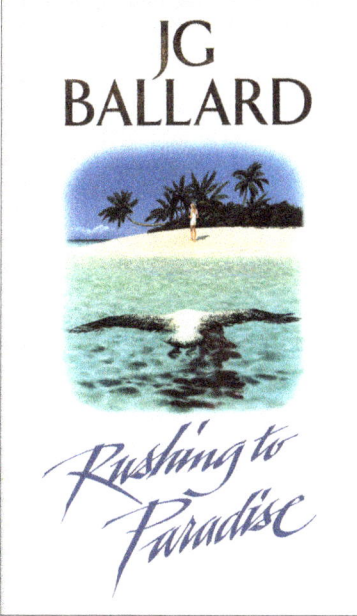

RUSHING TO PARADISE

UPRIGHT:
Meditate on the forgotten runways of
Wake Island, pointing towards the
Pacifics of your imagination

REVERSED:
Consider the lunacy of flowers,
the disease stored up for the human race
by the Apollo astronauts

III THE EMPRESS

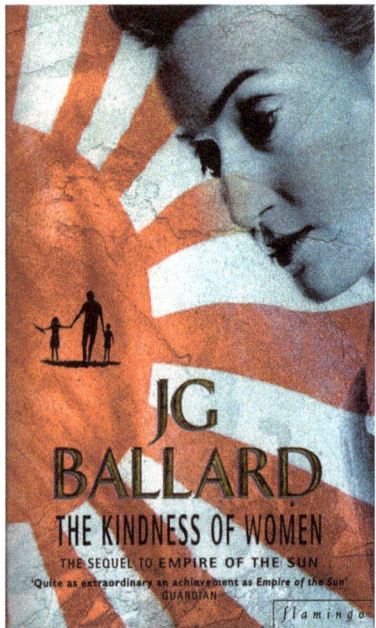

THE KINDNESS OF WOMEN

UPRIGHT:
Believe in adolescent women,
in their corruption by their own leg stances,
in the purity of their dishevelled bodies,
in the traces of their pudenda left in the
bathrooms of shabby motels

REVERSED:
Imagine the mysterious beauty of Margaret
Thatcher, the arch of her nostrils and
the sheen on her lower lip

IV THE EMPEROR

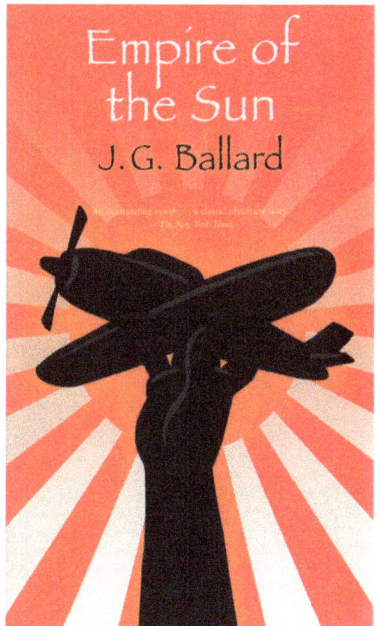

EMPIRE OF THE SUN

UPRIGHT:
Believe all reasons

REVERSED:
Imagine the loneliness of the sun,
the garrulousness of planets,
the repetitiveness of ourselves,
the inexistence of the universe
and the boredom of the atom

V THE HIEROPHANT

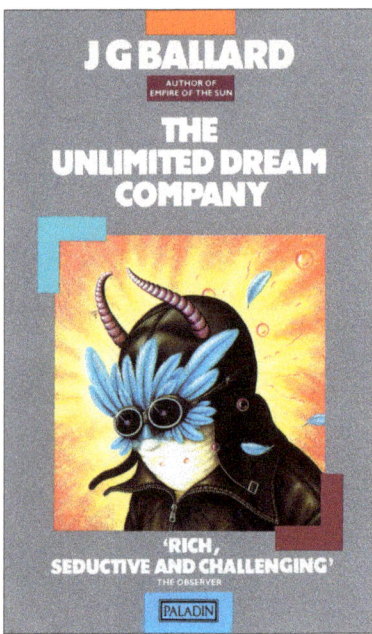

THE UNLIMITED DREAM COMPANY

UPRIGHT:
Contemplate flight, the beauty of the wing,
and the beauty of everything that has ever flown,
the stone thrown by a small child that carries
with it the wisdom of statesmen and midwives

REVERSED:
Focus on all hallucinations

VI THE LOVERS

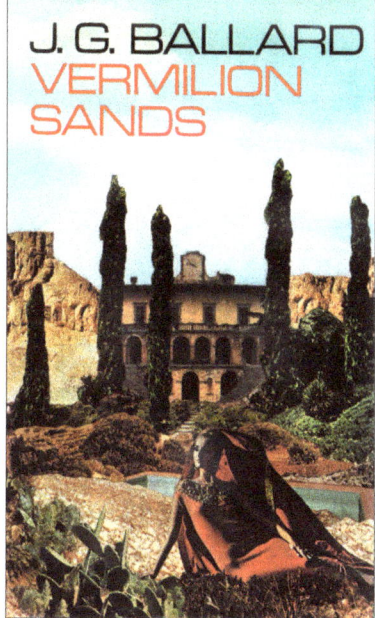

VERMILION SANDS

UPRIGHT:
Consider the death of tomorrow, the exhaustion
of time, your search for a new time within the
smiles of auto-route waitresses and the tired eyes
of air-traffic controllers at out-of-season airports

REVERSED:
Believe in the impossibility of existence,
in the humour of mountains,
in the absurdity of electromagnetism,
in the farce of geometry

VII THE CHARIOT

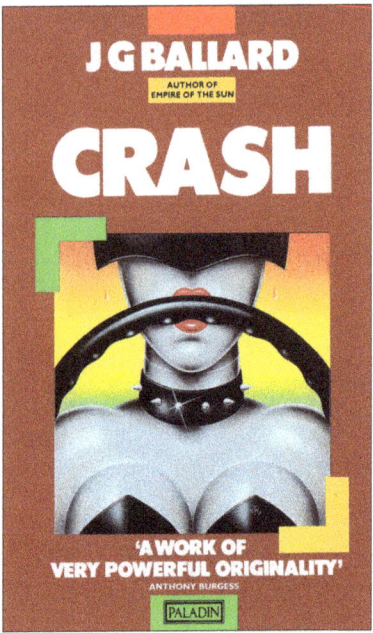

CRASH

UPRIGHT:
Follow your own obsessions,
the beauty of the car crash,
the peace of the submerged forest,
the excitements of the deserted holiday beach

REVERSED:
Listen to alcoholism, venereal disease,
fever and exhaustion.
Believe in pain

VIII STRENGTH

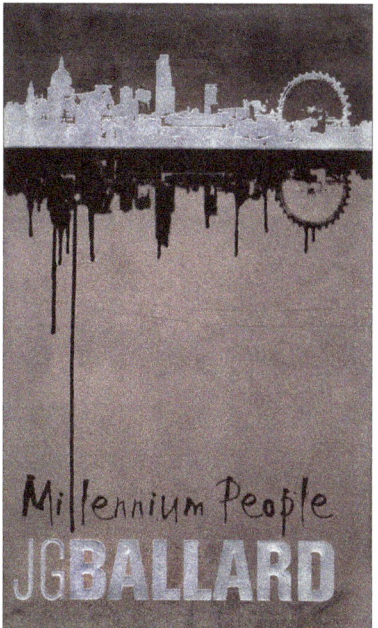

MILLENNIUM PEOPLE

UPRIGHT:
Be aware of the light cast by video-recorders in
department store windows,
the messianic insights of the radiator grilles
of showroom automobiles

REVERSED:
Remember the melancholy of wounded
Argentine conscripts; the haunted smiles of
filling station personnel

IX THE HERMIT

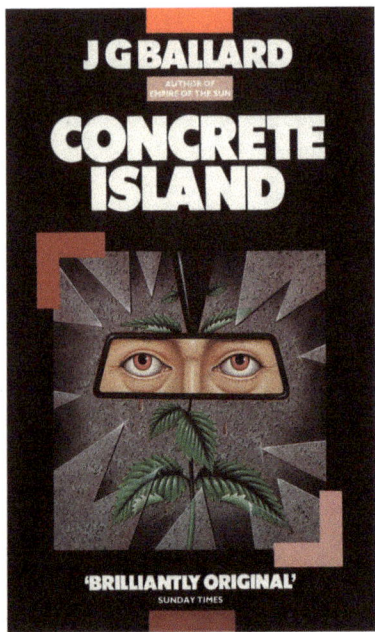

CONCRETE ISLAND

UPRIGHT:
Consider all excuses

REVERSED:
Believe in the death of the emotions
and the triumph of the imagination

X THE WHEEL OF FORTUNE

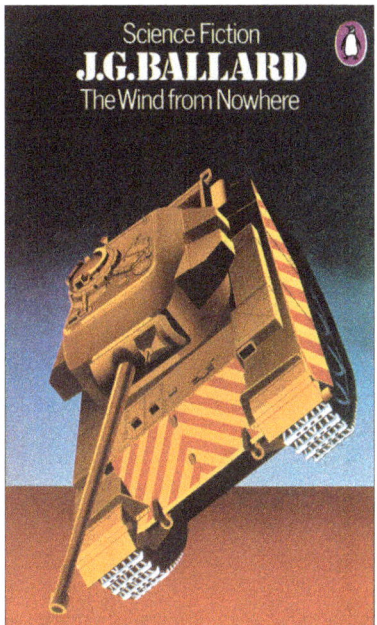

THE WIND FROM NOWHERE

UPRIGHT:
Consider the designers of the Pyramids,
the Empire State Building,
the Berlin Fuhrerbunker,
the Wake Island runways

REVERSED:
Believe in despair

XI JUSTICE

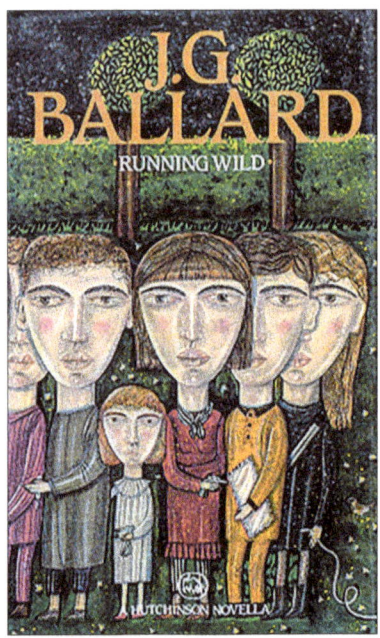

RUNNING WILD

UPRIGHT:
Believe in all children

REVERSED:
Remember all anger

XII THE HANGED MAN

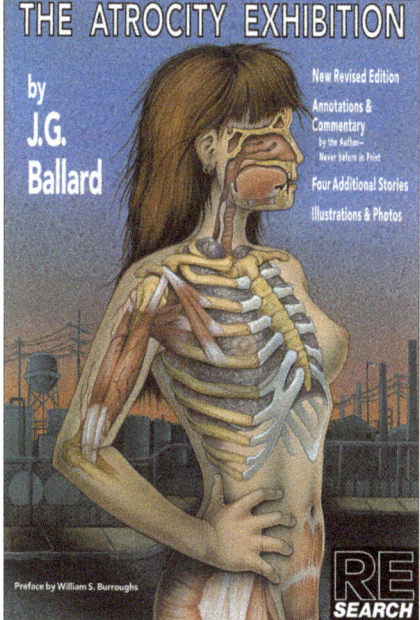

THE ATROCITY EXHIBITION

UPRIGHT:
Believe in the power of the imagination to
remake the world, to release the truth within us,
to hold back the night, to transcend death,
to ingratiate ourselves with birds

REVERSED:
Believe in anxiety, psychosis and despair

XIII DEATH

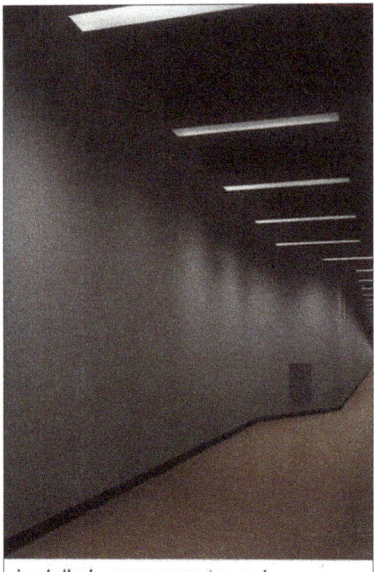

j. g. ballard - super-cannes / a novel

SUPER-CANNES

UPRIGHT:
Believe in the body odours of Princess Di

REVERSED:
Focus on a dream of Margaret Thatcher caressed by that young Argentine soldier in a forgotten motel watched by a tubercular filling station attendant

XIV TEMPERANCE

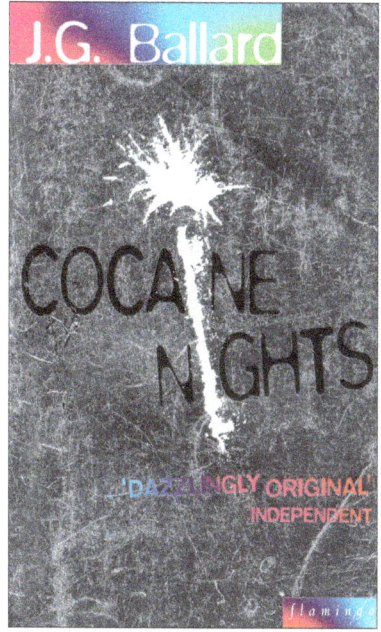

COCAINE NIGHTS

UPRIGHT:
Concentrate on maps, diagrams, codes,
chess-games, puzzles, airline time-tables,
airport indicator signs

REVERSED:
Focus on the derangement of the senses:
in Rimbaud, William Burroughs, Huysmans,
Genet, Celine, Swift, Defoe, Carroll,
Coleridge, Kafka

XV THE DEVIL

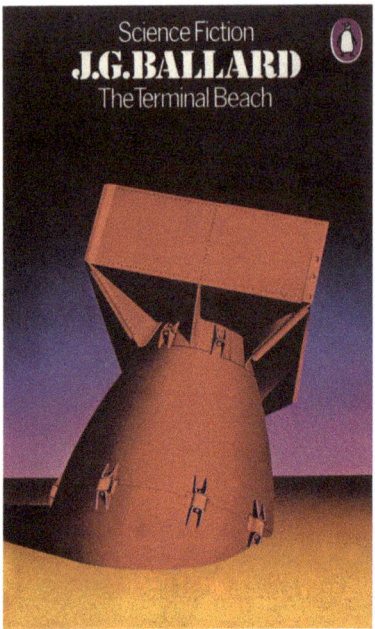

THE TEMINAL BEACH

UPRIGHT:
Listen to Tokyo, Benidorm, La Grande Motte,
Wake Island, Eniwetok, Dealey Plaza

REVERSED:
Consider the non-existence of the past,
the death of the future, and the infinite
possibilities of the present

XVI THE TOWER

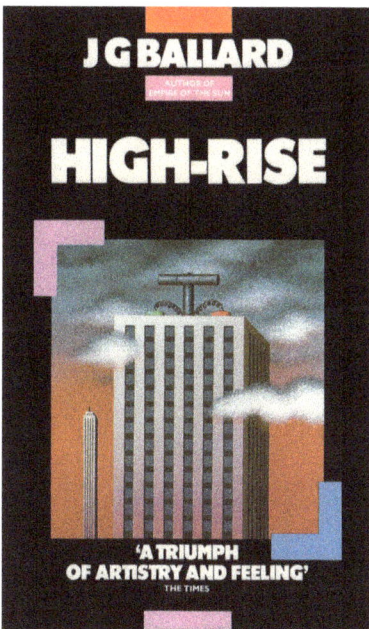

High-Rise

UPRIGHT:
See the genital organs of great men and women,
the body postures of Reagan,
Thatcher and Princess Di,
the sweet odours emanating from their lips as
they regard the cameras of the entire world

REVERSED:
Believe in madness, in the truth of the
inexplicable, in the common sense of stones

XVII THE STAR

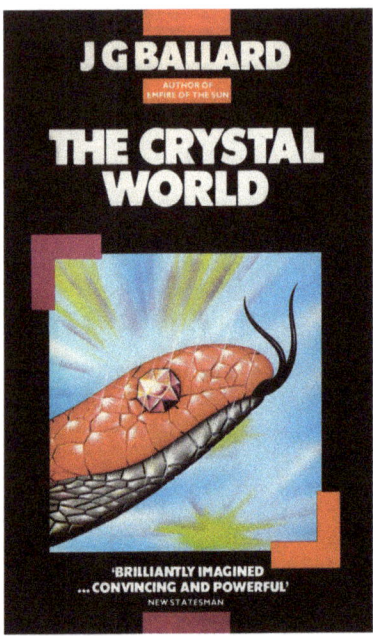

The Crystal World

UPRIGHT:
Believe in the mystery and melancholy
of a hand, in the kindness of trees,
the wisdom of light

REVERSED:
Search out the cruelty of arithmetic,
the murderous intent of logic

XVIII THE MOON

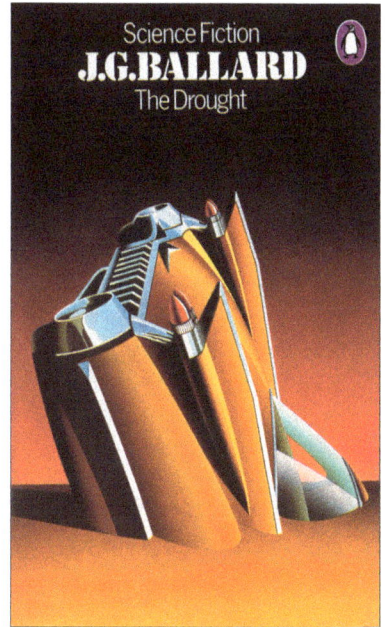

THE DROUGHT

UPRIGHT:
Search out the elegance of the oil stains
on the engine nacelles of 747s
parked on airport tarmacs

REVERSED:
Be aware of the history of your feet

XIX THE SUN

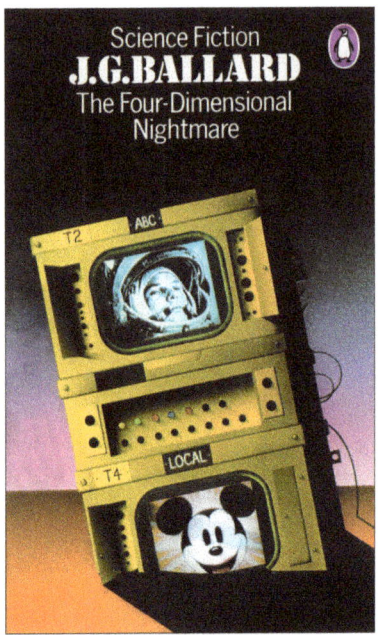

THE 4-DIMENSIONAL NIGHTMARE

UPRIGHT:
Imagine the next five minutes

REVERSED:
Remember migraines,
the boredom of afternoons,
the fear of calendars,
the treachery of clocks

XX JUDGEMENT

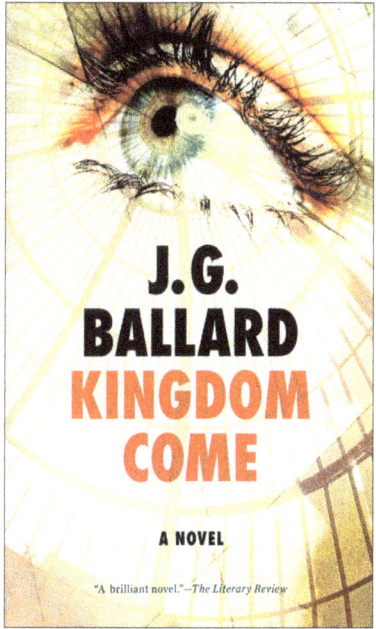

Kingdom Come

UPRIGHT:
Focus on the junction of disenchanted bodies
with the enchanted chromium rails
of supermarket counters; their warm tolerance
of your own perversions

REVERSED:
Believe in the gentleness of the surgeon's knife,
the limitless geometry of the cinema screen,
the hidden universe within supermarkets

XXI THE WORLD

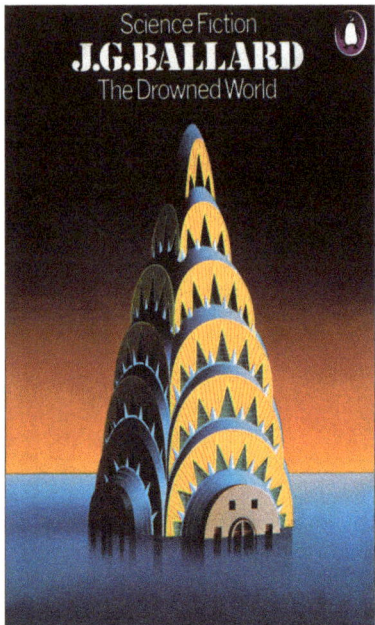

THE DROWNED WORLD

UPRIGHT:
Remember Max Ernst, Delvaux, Dali, Titian,
Goya, Leonardo, Vermeer, Chirico, Magritte,
Redon, Durer, Tanguy, the Facteur Cheval,
the Watts Towers, Bocklin, Francis Bacon

REVERSED:
Consider all the invisible artists within the
psychiatric institutions of the planet

CARD	UPRIGHT	REVERSED
0 THE FOOL	Contemplate the elegance of automobile graveyards, the mystery of multi-storey car parks, the poetry of abandoned hotels	Move towards mythologies, memories, lies, fantasies, evasions
I THE MAGICIAN	Be aware of the beauty of all women, the treachery of their imaginations, so close to your heart	Contemplate the perversions, the infatuations with trees, princesses, prime ministers, derelict filling stations (more beautiful than the Taj Mahal), clouds and birds
II THE HIGH PRIESTESS	Meditate on the forgotten runways of Wake Island, pointing towards the Pacifics of your imagination	Consider the lunacy of flowers, the disease stored up for the human race by the Apollo Astronauts
III THE EMPRESS	Believe in adolescent women, in their corruption by their own leg stances, in the purity of their dishevelled bodies, in the traces of their pudenda left in the bathrooms of shabby motels	Imagine the mysterious beauty of Margaret Thatcher, the arch of her nostrils and the sheen on her lower lip
IV THE EMPEROR	Believe all reasons	Imagine the loneliness of the sun, the garrulousness of planets, the repetitiveness of ourselves, the inexistence of the universe and the boredom of the atom
V THE HIEROPHANT	Contemplate flight, the beauty of the wing, and the beauty of everything that has ever flown, the stone thrown by a small child that carries with it the wisdom of statesmen and midwives	Focus on all hallucinations
VI THE LOVERS	Consider the death of tomorrow, the exhaustion of time, your search for a new time within the smiles of auto-route waitresses and the tired eyes of air-traffic controllers at out-of-season airports	Believe in the impossibility of existence, in the humour of mountains, in the absurdity of electromagnetism, in the farce of geometry

CARD	UPRIGHT	REVERSED
VII THE CHARIOT	Follow your own obsessions, the beauty of the car crash, the peace of the submerged forest, the excitements of the deserted holiday beach	Listen to alcoholism, venereal disease, fever and exhaustion. Believe in pain
VIII STRENGTH	Be aware of the light cast by video-recorders in department store windows, the messianic insights of the radiator grilles of showroom automobiles	Remember the melancholy of wounded Argentine conscripts; the haunted smiles of filling station personnel
IX THE HERMIT	Consider all excuses	Believe in the death of the emotions and the triumph of the imagination
X THE WHEEL OF FORTUNE	Consider the designers of the Pyramids, the Empire State Building, the Berlin Fuhrerbunker, the Wake Island runways	Believe in despair
XI JUSTICE	Believe in all children	Remember all anger
XII THE HANGED MAN	Believe in the power of the imagination to remake the world, to release the truth within us, to hold back the night, to transcend death, to ingratiate ourselves with birds	Believe in anxiety, psychosis and despair
XIII DEATH	Believe in the body odours of Princess Di	Focus on a dream of Margaret Thatcher caressed by that young Argentine soldier in a forgotten motel watched by a tubercular filling station attendant
XIV TEMPERANCE	Concentrate on maps, diagrams, codes, chess-games, puzzles, airline time-tables, airport indicator signs	Focus on the derangement of the senses: in Rimbaud, William Burroughs, Huysmans, Genet, Celine, Swift, Defoe, Carroll, Coleridge, Kafka

CARD	UPRIGHT	REVERSED
XV THE DEVIL	Listen to Tokyo, Benidorm, La Grande Motte, Wake Island, Eniwetok, Dealey Plaza	Consider the non-existence of the past, the death of the future, and the infinite possibilities of the present
XVI THE TOWER	See the genital organs of great men and women, the body postures of Reagan, Thatcher and Princess Di, the sweet odours emanating from their lips as they regard the cameras of the entire world	Believe in madness, in the truth of the inexplicable, in the common sense of stones
XVII THE STAR	Believe in the mystery and melancholy of a hand, in the kindness of trees, the wisdom of light	Search out the cruelty of arithmetic, the murderous intent of logic
XVIII THE MOON	Search out the elegance of the oil stains on the engine nacelles of 747s parked on airport tarmacs	Be aware of the history of your feet
XIX THE SUN	Imagine the next five minutes	Remember migraines, the boredom of afternoons, the fear of calendars, the treachery of clocks
XX JUDGEMENT	Focus on the junction of disenchanted bodies with the enchanted chromium rails of supermarket counters; their warm tolerance of your own perversions	Believe in the gentleness of the surgeon's knife, the limitless geometry of the cinema screen, the hidden universe within supermarkets
XXI THE WORLD	Remember Max Ernst, Delvaux, Dali, Titian, Goya, Leonardo, Vermeer, Chirico, Magritte, Redon, Durer, Tanguy, the Facteur Cheval, the Watts Towers, Bocklin, Francis Bacon	Consider all the invisible artists within the psychiatric institutions of the planet

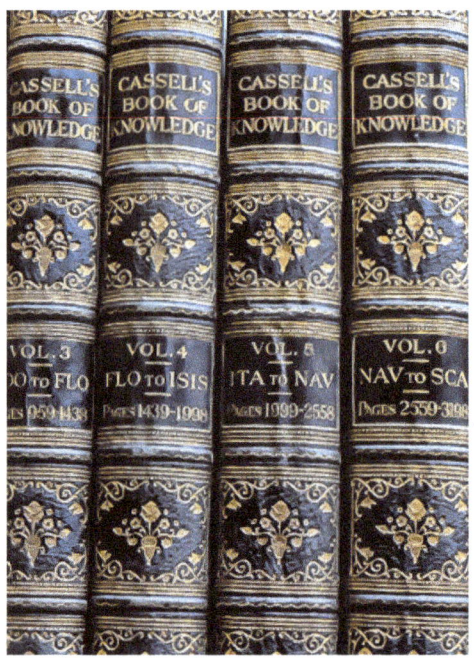

JG Ballard's Book of Knowledge

Ballard believed in the Waverley because he had read it as a boy. Whenever he was bored his mother had told him, "Go and read 'The Eight Volumes.' That was her name for them," he chuckles. "It was the nearest thing to television."

Marianne Brace interviewing JG Ballard, *Independent*, 15 September 2006

'I sold encyclopaedias door to door, a job at which I was surprisingly successful, partly because the Waverley encyclopaedia was the one I had read as a child in Shanghai —I knew it backwards and genuinely believed in it ... and I often waived my commission ... to secure for them the hours of intelligent pleasure I had known as a child.

JG Ballard's memoir *Miracles of Life*, 2008

Cassell & Co publishers created the Waverley Book Company in 1909 to distribute deluxe editions. One of their most successful products was the eight volume *Book of Knowledge*, the beloved encyclopaedia Ballard talks about above.

We can't be sure exactly which edition the Ballard family owned in the 1930s, but it was probably very similar to the edition photographed opposite, which is undated, but internal evidence suggests it was produced in the 1920s.

As it is out of copyright, I made a complete searchable facsimile of the *Book of Knowledge* to explore the articles and images that so enraptured and enthused the young Ballard.

It's interesting to note that in 1992, Cassell & Co bought Victor Gollancz Ltd, Ballard's first British book publisher. (Thanks to David Pringle for that and other helpful leads.)

The colour plates are worth particular scrutiny, sumptuous and kitsch, they speak of an empire at the height of its pomp.

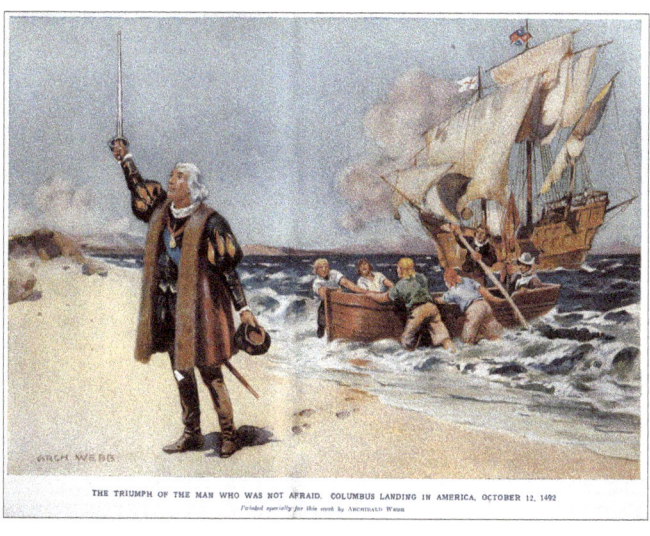

THE TRIUMPH OF THE MAN WHO WAS NOT AFRAID. COLUMBUS LANDING IN AMERICA, OCTOBER 12, 1492

We see Christopher Columbus landing on the welcoming sands of America, a place he never reached in reality. There are echoes of *Hello America* and other doomed Ballardian journeys.

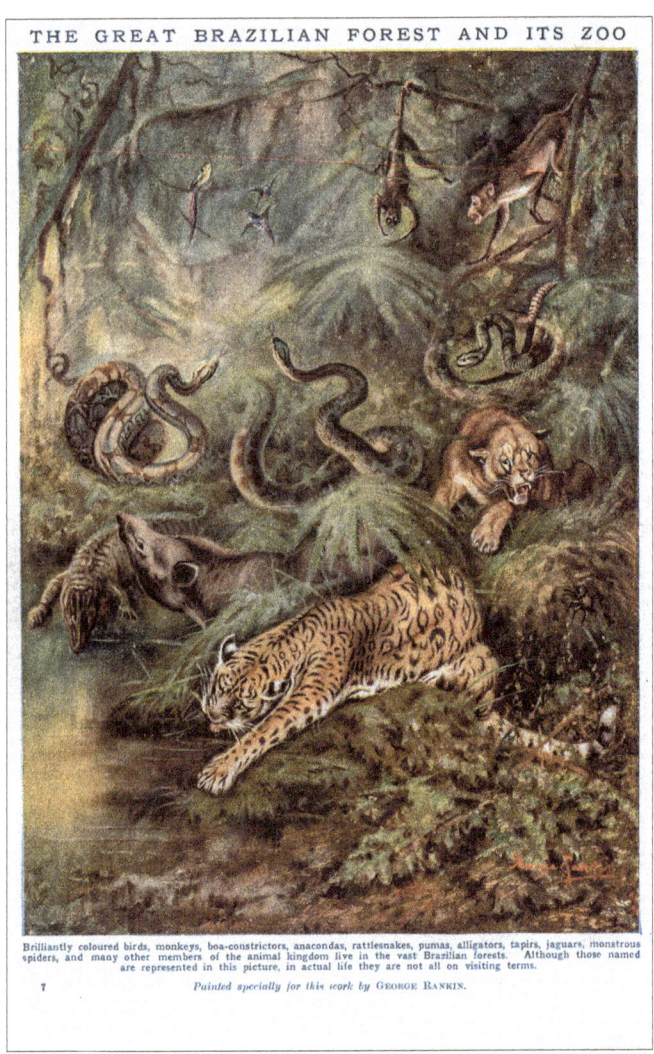

THE GREAT BRAZILIAN FOREST AND ITS ZOO

Brilliantly coloured birds, monkeys, boa-constrictors, anacondas, rattlesnakes, pumas, alligators, tapirs, jaguars, monstrous spiders, and many other members of the animal kingdom live in the vast Brazilian forests. Although those named are represented in this picture, in actual life they are not all on visiting terms.

Painted specially for this work by GEORGE RANKIN.

There are wild animals aplenty in Ballard's mental jungles, such as *The Day of Creation* and *Rushing to Paradise*.

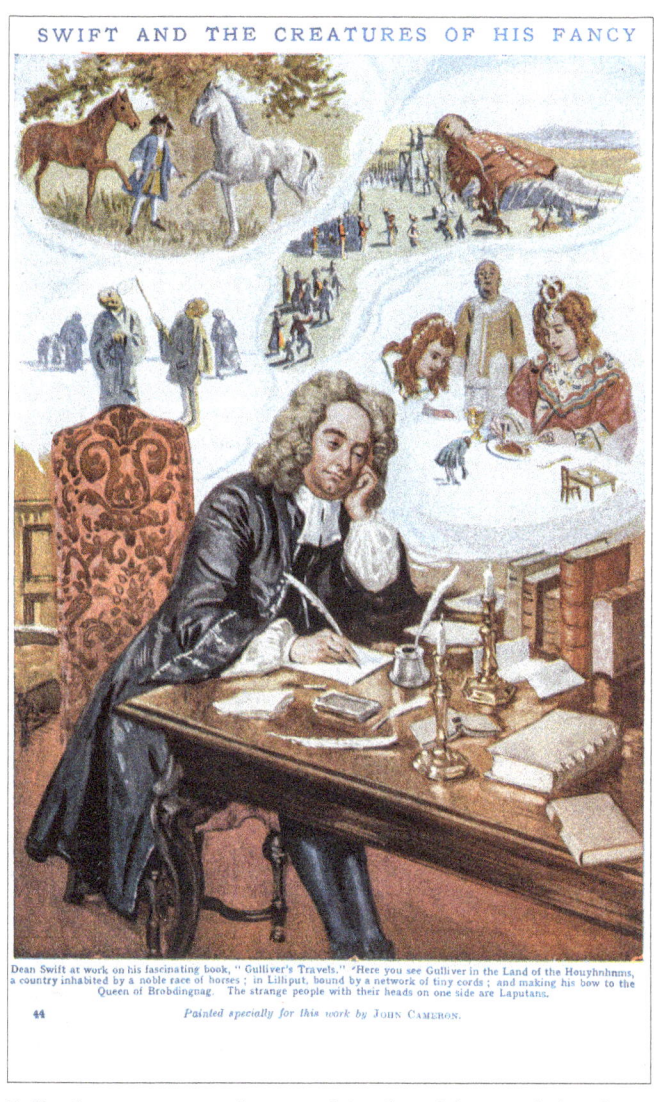

Dean Swift at work on his fascinating book, "Gulliver's Travels." "Here you see Gulliver in the Land of the Houyhnhnms, a country inhabited by a noble race of horses; in Lilliput, bound by a network of tiny cords; and making his bow to the Queen of Brobdingnag. The strange people with their heads on one side are Laputans.

Painted specially for this work by JOHN CAMERON.

Ballard was a great admirer of Swift and his work has been compared with that of the great satirist. We can see in the dream of Gulliver above a foreshadowing of *The Drowned Giant*.

A SWIFT FIGHTING GIANT OF THE BRITISH NAVY

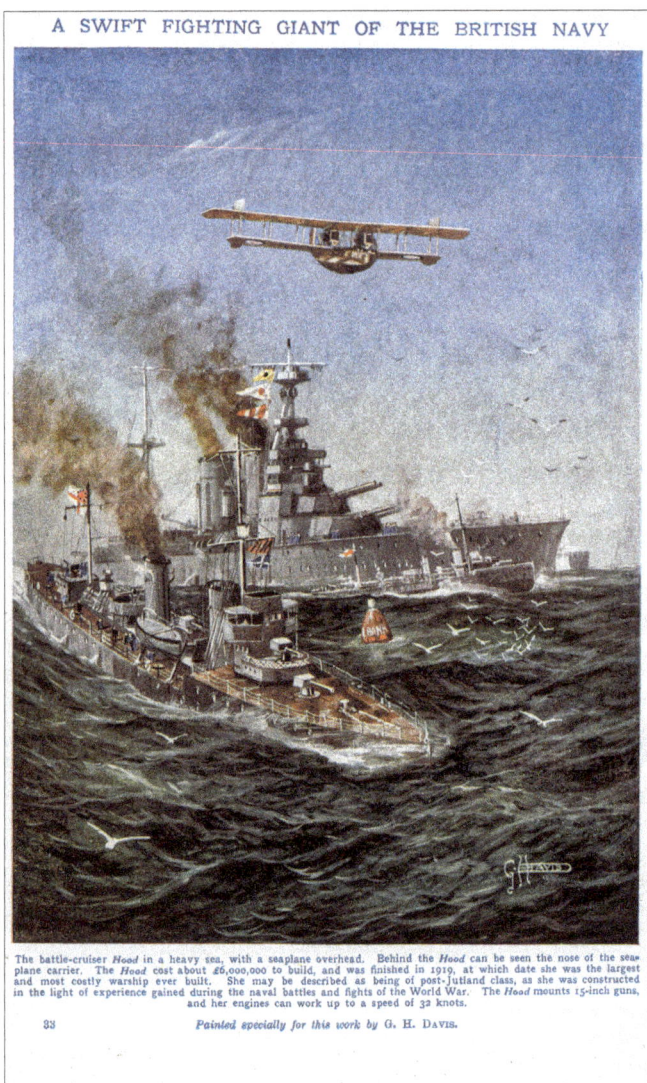

The battle-cruiser *Hood* in a heavy sea, with a seaplane overhead. Behind the *Hood* can be seen the nose of the seaplane carrier. The *Hood* cost about £6,000,000 to build, and was finished in 1919, at which date she was the largest and most costly warship ever built. She may be described as being of post-Jutland class, as she was constructed in the light of experience gained during the naval battles and fights of the World War. The *Hood* mounts 15-inch guns, and her engines can work up to a speed of 32 knots.

Painted specially for this work by G. H. Davis.

Ballard was ever aware of the enormous might yet inherent fragility of the Empire.

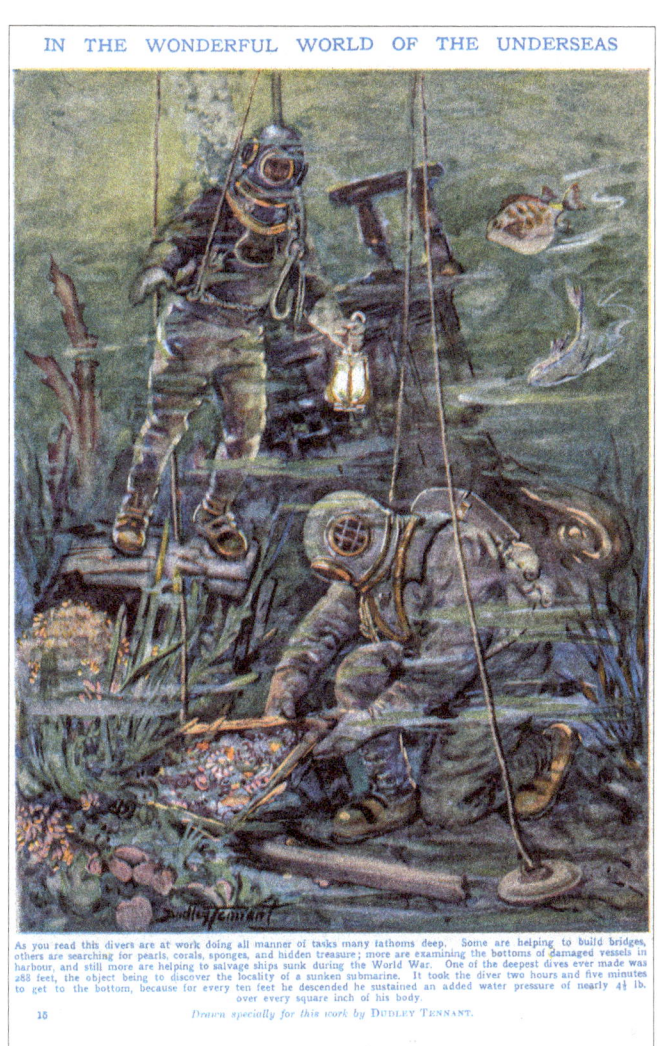

IN THE WONDERFUL WORLD OF THE UNDERSEAS

As you read this divers are at work doing all manner of tasks many fathoms deep. Some are helping to build bridges, others are searching for pearls, corals, sponges, and hidden treasure; more are examining the bottoms of damaged vessels in harbour, and still more are helping to salvage ships sunk during the World War. One of the deepest dives ever made was 288 feet, the object being to discover the locality of a sunken submarine. It took the diver two hours and five minutes to get to the bottom, because for every ten feet he descended he sustained an added water pressure of nearly 4¼ lb. over every square inch of his body.

Drawn specially for this work by DUDLEY TENNANT.

This image could almost be an illustration for *The Drowned World*.

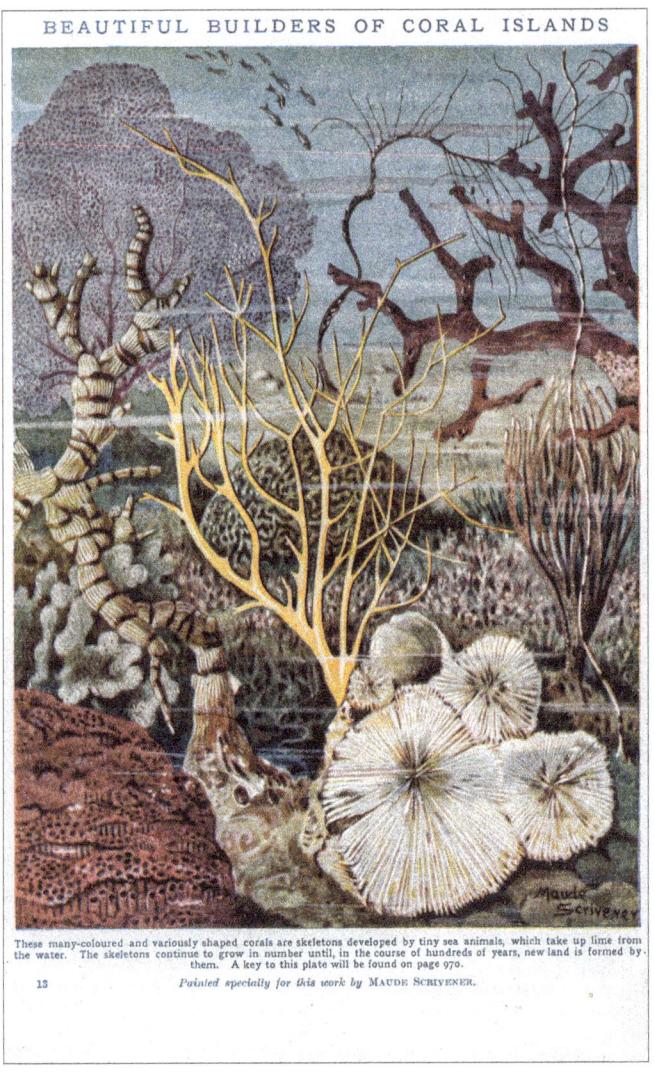

BEAUTIFUL BUILDERS OF CORAL ISLANDS

These many-coloured and variously shaped corals are skeletons developed by tiny sea animals, which take up lime from the water. The skeletons continue to grow in number until, in the course of hundreds of years, new land is formed by them. A key to this plate will be found on page 970.

Painted specially for this work by MAUDE SCRIVENER.

… and again the mysterious underwater world that so fascinated Ballard.

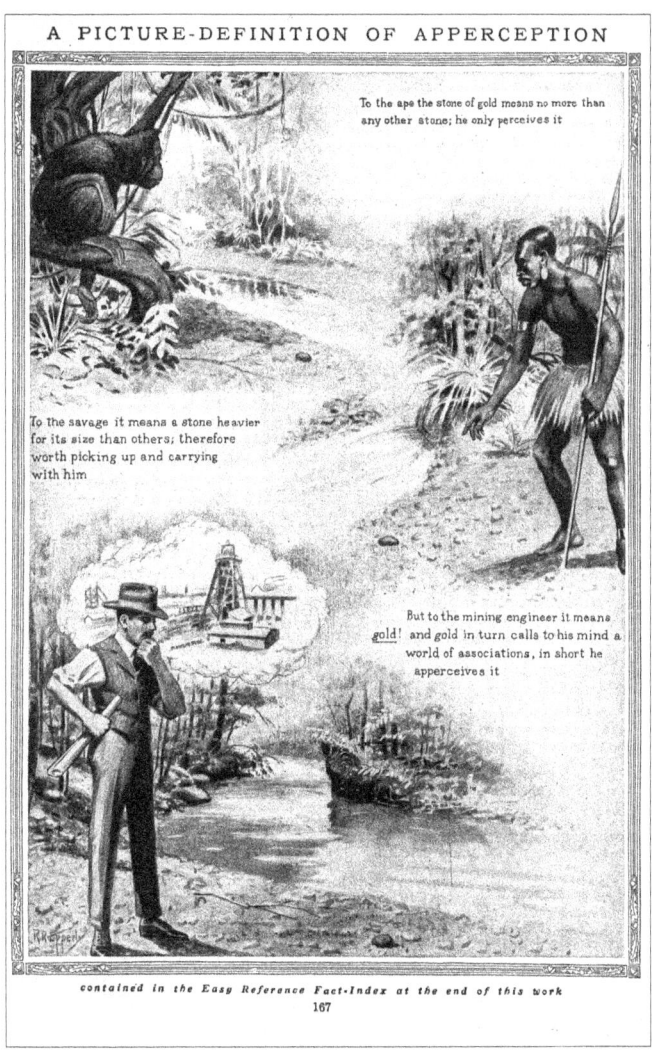

Ballard's encyclopedia, like the rest of the society he was born into, was inherently racist.

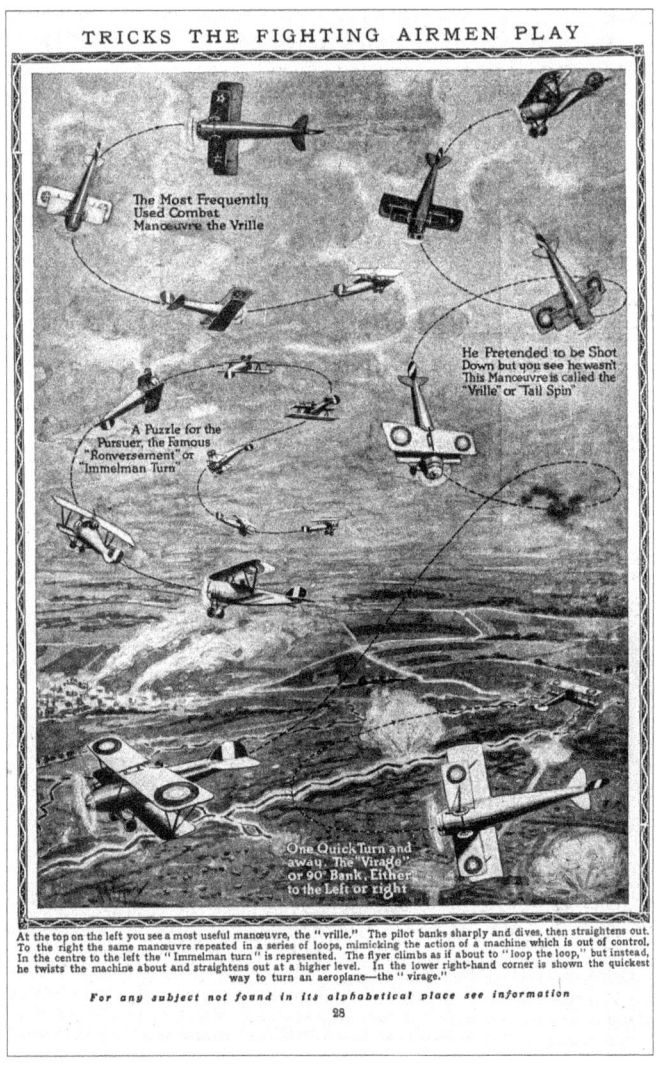

The young Ballard's love of flight might have been fed by images like this.

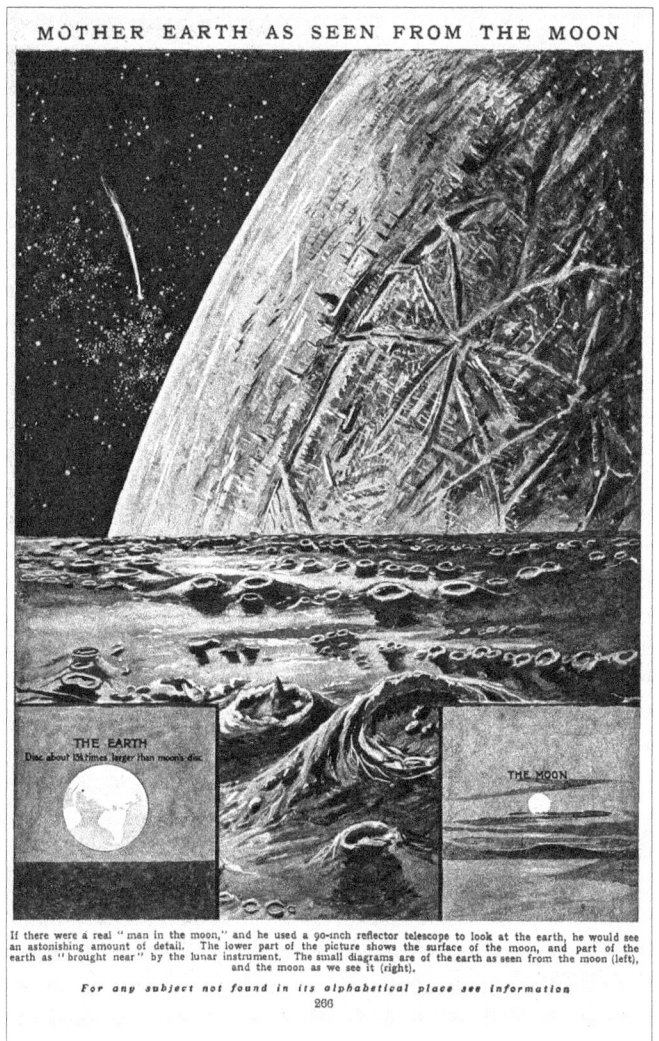

The Encyclopedia encouraged astronomical speculation.

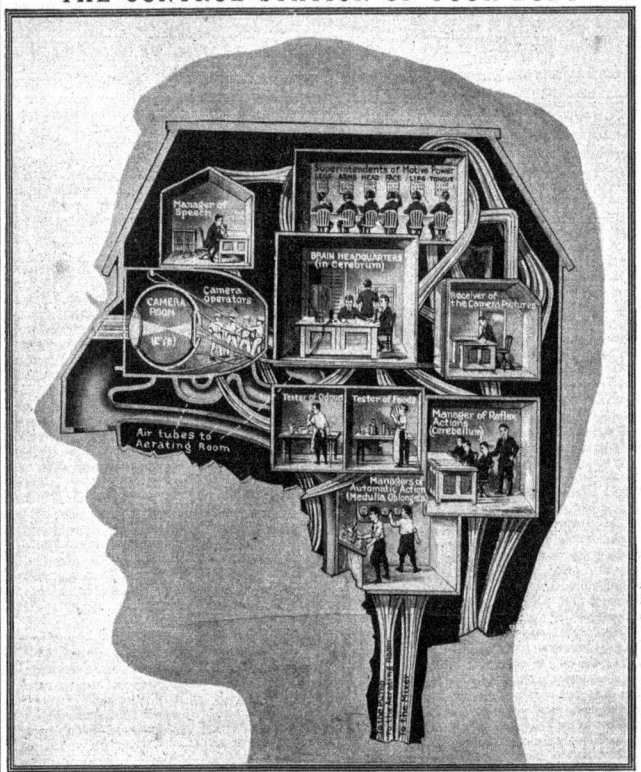

... as well as more fanciful psychology.

| MOTOR-CARS | | The Wonderful Differential |

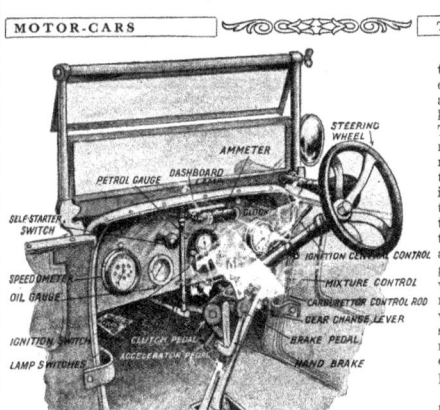

Fig. 7.—Dashboard, with left-hand control.

To get over this difficulty there is introduced the differential or balance gear. The axle is cut into halves, each half ending with a gear-wheel. These two gear-wheels are in mesh with a third wheel at right angles to them, and all three wheels are contained in a casing. The drive from the gear-shaft is applied *outside* this casing. In other words, the two halves of the shaft and their central connecting gear are driven round as a whole, but when the car reaches a bend or turn each wheel can assume just the speed that is necessary at the moment. Either rear wheel of a car can be rotated independently of the other.

Suspend a car in the air; grip one wheel and get somebody else to turn the other. What happens? The gears in the gear-box are rotated. Do not grip one wheel, but turn either of them. What happens? Both wheels turn, *but in opposite directions*.

—but it is always necessary to have a change-speed gear, because of road contingencies which may be met with at any moment. There is promise, one of these days, of a car in which all mechanical-reduction gearing will be omitted, and the engine itself will be relied upon to give every variation of speed required.

The power is transmitted by a shaft from gear-box to the back axle. Here is one of the most baffling pieces of mechanism known to engineering. It is the "differential" gear. Watch some men at drill and see them obey the order: "Left wheel!" The pivot man remains almost stationary whilst the outer man marches through a space equal to a quarter of a circle.

Now apply this simple lesson to the back wheels of a car. Suppose both wheels are absolutely fixed to their axle and that their axle is in some way driven by a shaft extending from the gear-box. Everything is all right while the car is moving in a straight line, but on coming to a sharp bend one wheel must go faster than the other.

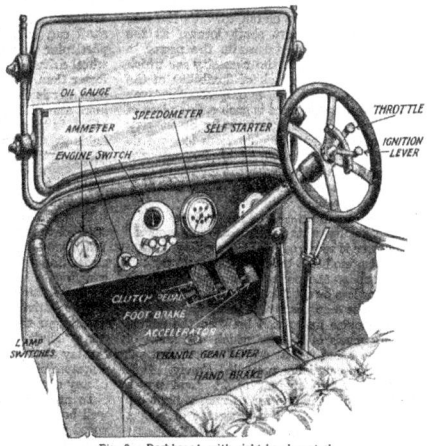

Fig. 8.—Dashboard, with right-hand control.

For any subject not found in its alphabetical place see information
2492

There are extensive details of mechanical marvels,

109

| SHANGHAI | | SHANTUNG |

SHANGHAI', CHINA. The European city, in which collect merchants, missionaries, and adventurers from all the countries of the world, is clean and handsome, with splendid shops and houses, broad streets, and many trees. The Chinese city, in which herd nearly a million Chinese, is unbelievably dirty and squalid. Each city is distinct, with its own boundaries, government, and courts, so that foreigners are not subject to the laws of China.

A Medley of Races

The streets of the "international settlement," policed by black-bearded Sikhs from India, are scarcely less colourful than those of the native city, where Chinese from every province in the country come to transact business. Nowhere is Shanghai's strange medley of races better shown than along the wide Bund or waterfront, where European taxicabs, carts drawn by Mongolian ponies, and Chinese rickshaws, sedan-chairs, and wheelbarrows await their fares.

The great productiveness of the country around Shanghai and its strategic position at the mouth of the Yangtze, China's greatest river, make it one of the most important seaports in the Far East. Railways lead inland from Shanghai, and 40 miles away is the Grand Canal, China's great waterway between north and south. By these routes come for export a vast amount of tea, rice, cotton, wool, beans, wheat, silk, and hides. Chief among the imports are cotton, yarns, and cloth, coal, sugar, metals, machinery, and oil. Shanghai has a larger commerce than all other Chinese ports. Population, about 1,500,000.

SHANTUNG (*shän-tung'*), CHINA. On the east coast of China, looking across the Yellow Sea to Korea and Japan, lies Shantung—a mountainous promontory 100 miles wide and 200 long, reaching out from the alluvial plains built of the silt brought down by the treacherous Hwang-ho or Yellow River. Into this province are crowded 25,000,000 Chinese. It is the land of "shantung" and of "pongee" silk, made from the wild silkworm cocoons. Silk, coal, and iron, and the "coolie" labourer constitute its chief sources of wealth.

In 1897-98 Germany acquired a concession of territory in Shantung—the bay of Kiaochow and fishing village of Tsingtau—as a penalty for the killing of two German missionaries. Shortly after Weihaiwei, on the north coast of the promontory, was leased to England.

Falls under German Control

Tsingtau became a great port and military and commercial centre, and the whole province came largely under German economic control. Other cities were modernized, including Tsinan, the capital, and railways were built with German capital to connect them. The mining operations, begun by Germany and continued by Japan, are still in the early stages of development, but the presence of coal and iron together with a large supply of cheap labour give promise that Shantung will become one of the chief iron and steel centres of eastern Asia.

In payment for her capture of Kiaochow during the World War Japan demanded of China, and was given by the Peace of Versailles, the German economic concessions in Shantung —i.e. railways, mines of all sorts, submarine

THE FORMER GERMAN CITY OF KIAOCHOW

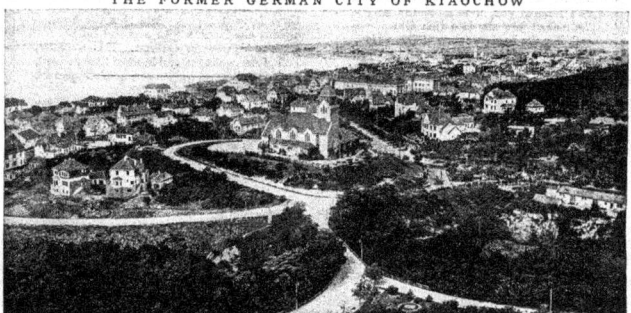

This neat little garden city, with its trim modern houses, was built by the Germans when they acquired their Shantung concession in 1898. After the World War it passed under Japanese control, but has since been returned to China. It was from this port that 150,000 Chinese coolies embarked for France during the World War.

For any subject not found in its alphabetical place see information

3264

… but less detail about Ballard's home town, the 'European city' of Shanghai.

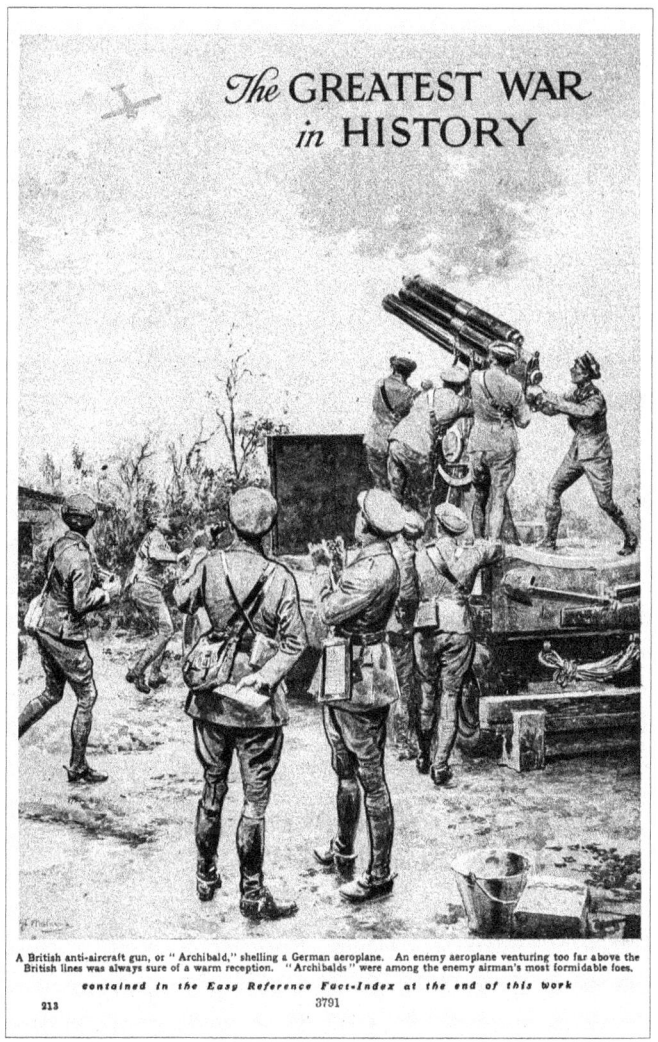

There were also foreshadowings of things to come …

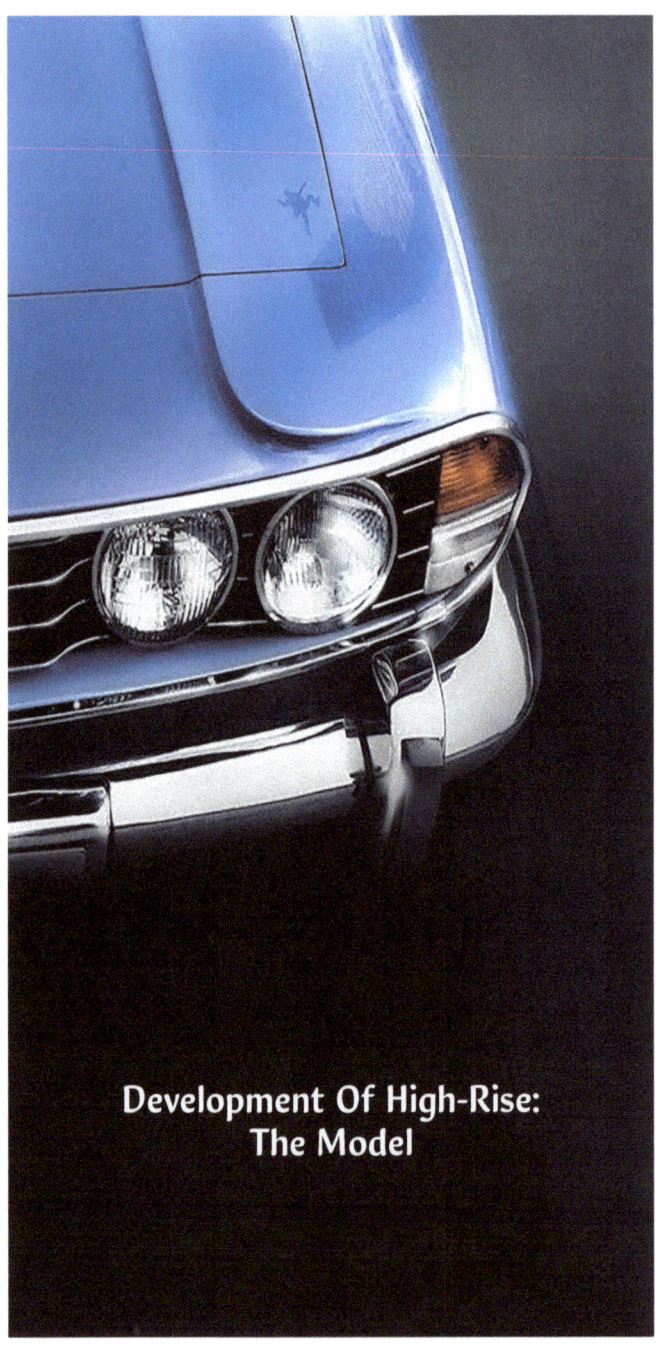

Development Of High-Rise:
The Model

In 2012 I was excited by the news there was to be a film made of Ballard's novel *High-Rise*—this turned out to be Ben Wheatley's excellent *High-Rise* (2015). I wanted to know if Ballard's very specific vision of a building could be accurately modelled.

> "With its forty floors and thousand apartments, its supermarket and swimming-pools, bank and junior school—all in effect abandoned in the sky—the high-rise offered more than enough opportunities for violence and confrontation. ...
>
> "For all its size, the high-rise contained an impressive range of services. The entire 10th floor was given over to a wide concourse, as large as an aircraft carrier's flight-deck, which contained a supermarket, bank and hairdressing salon, a swimming-pool and gymnasium, a well-stocked liquor store and a junior school for the few young children in the block. High above Laing, on the 35th floor, was a second, smaller swimming-pool, a sauna and a restaurant. Delighted by this glut of conveniences, Laing made less and less effort to leave the building."
> —From Ballard's *High-Rise* (1975)

I turned to SketchUp, a free 3D architecture application, to see if Ballard's mental model of the building could be made concrete.

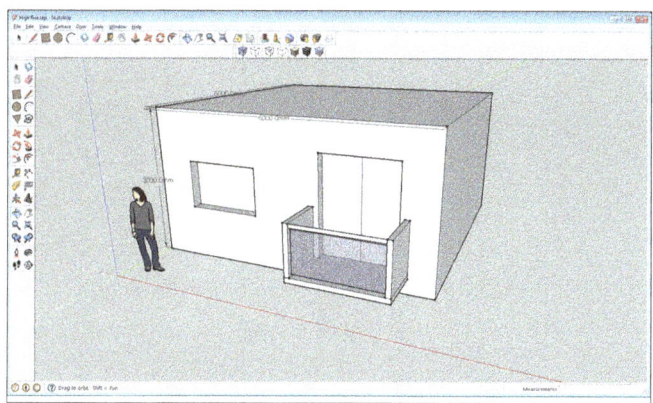

It was challenging to fit 1,000 apartments into a forty-storey building, but Ballard indicates the lower floors have relatively tiny units.

Copying and slotting together units was relatively straightforward.

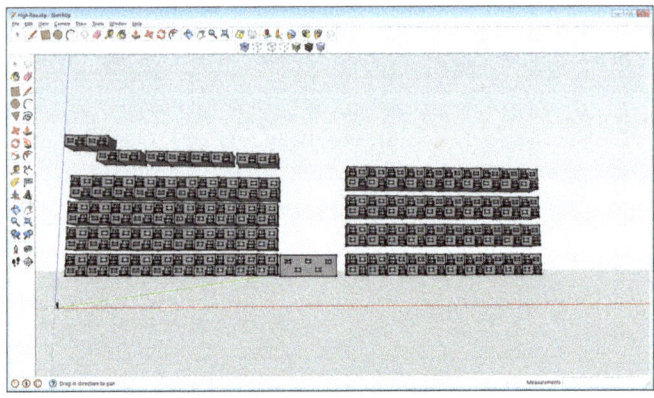

The apartments do get larger in the higher floors, topped by the luxurious penthouse owned by the architect Royal, echoing the way Ernö Goldfinger briefly lived in a flat at the top of his Balfron Tower.

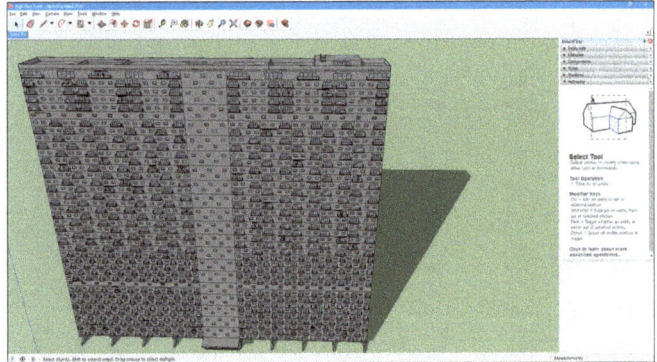

Ben Wheatley's early storyboards of the High-Rise show a similarity to this model.

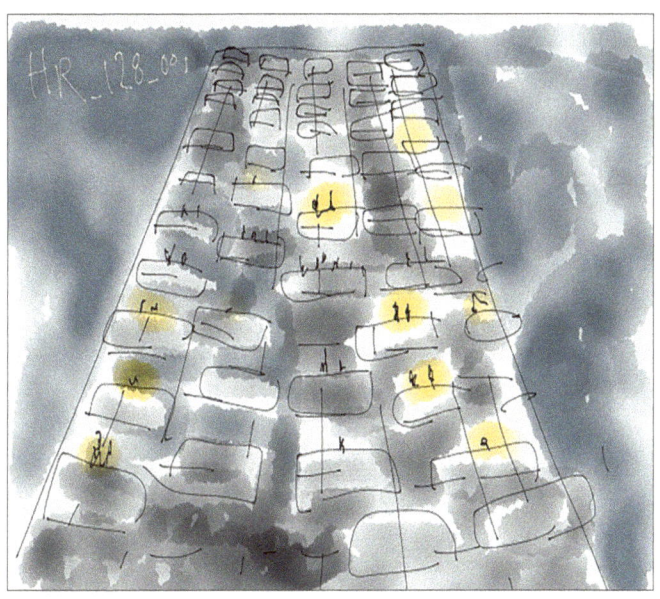

… as do early digital mock ups

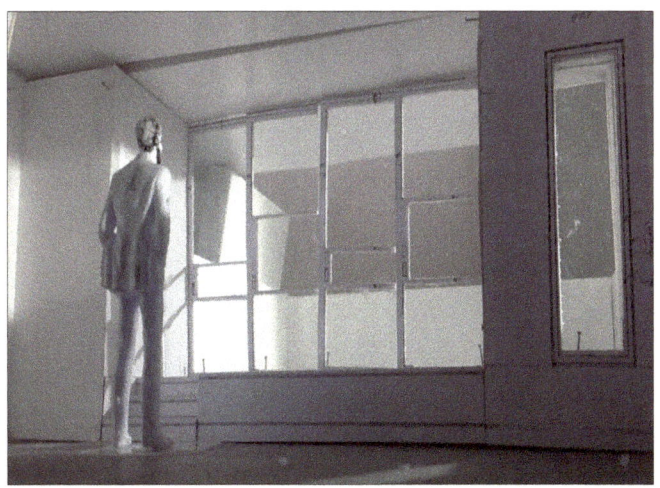

But the final CGI images were much more impressive.

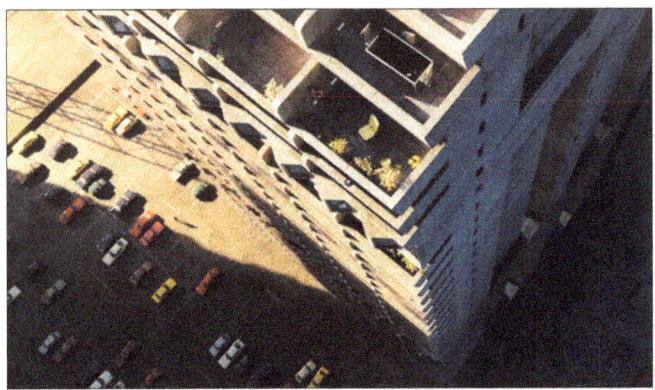

I wanted to link my model back to the original text, so took the phrases where Ballard mentioned specific floors and projected them onto the appropriate apartments.

I moved a virtual camera between them in the order they occurred in the text and made my own 10 minute movie of *High-Rise*: https://www.youtube.com/watch?v=uox33zvCNyA

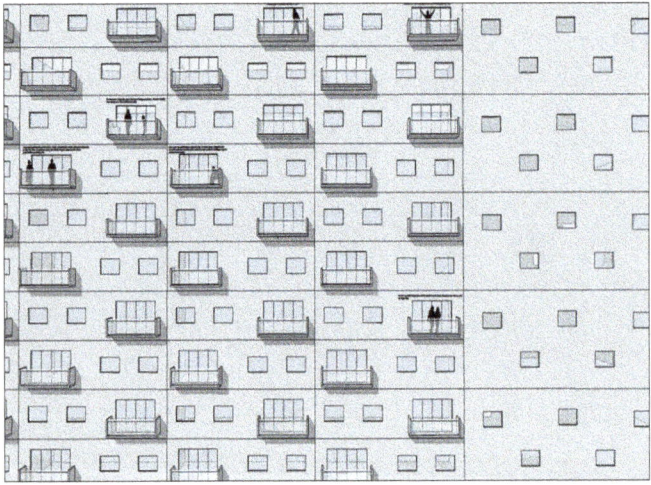

Here are some highlights:

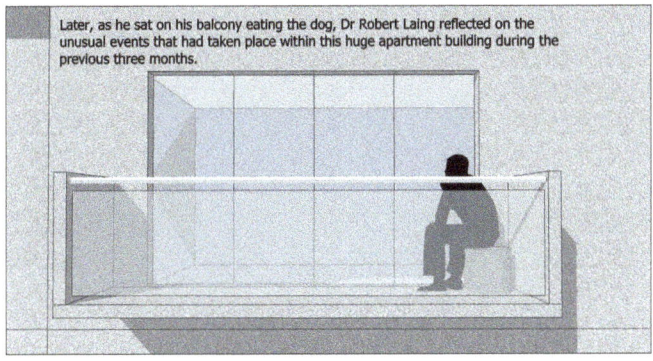

One of the most memorable opening lines in literature. Ballard lets us know from the start that this is no ordinary story.

As I developed the model, I became more aware of the spatial relationships between the protagonists. The closeness of neighbours and the gulfs between the classes.

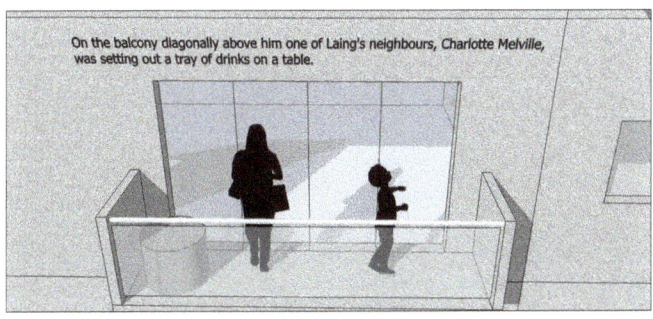

Balconies provide routes of communication and conflict.

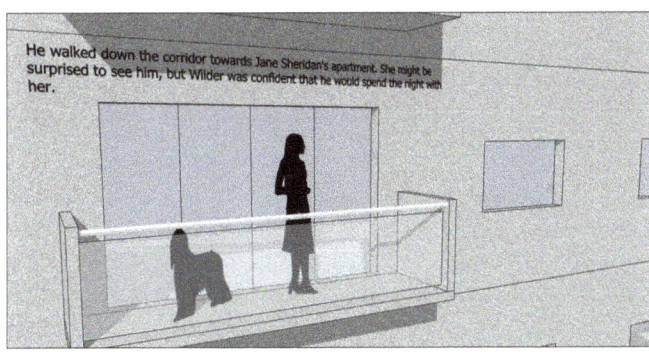

The honeycombed flats provide opportunities for both isolation and intimacy.

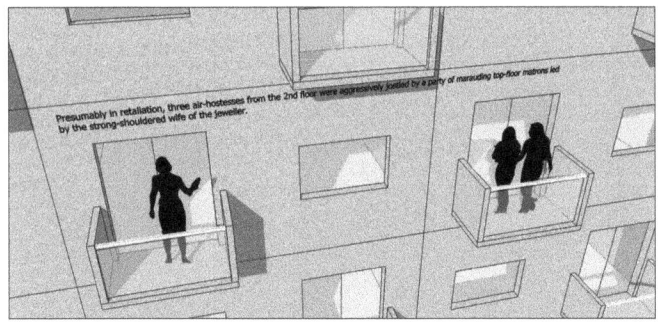

The lifts and foyers can be rallying points or zones of conflict.

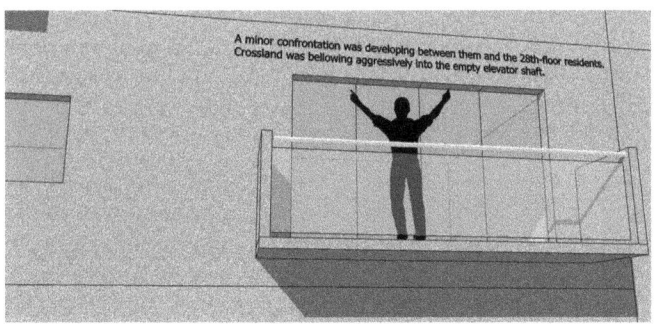

The High-Rise is the embodiment of the theory that bad buildings make people bad. Ballard adds a unique twist to this trope. The residents come to enjoy their madness and don't want anyone from outside interfering in it.

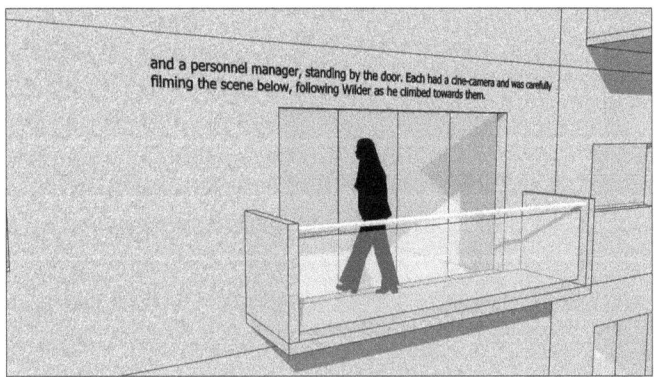

They film their derangement but lie to the authorities about it.

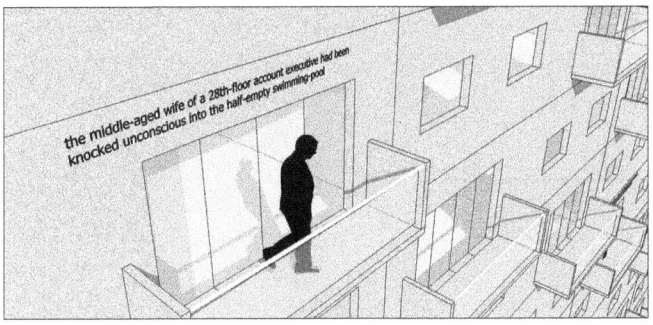

The society in the High-Rise splinters into new, more violent groupings.

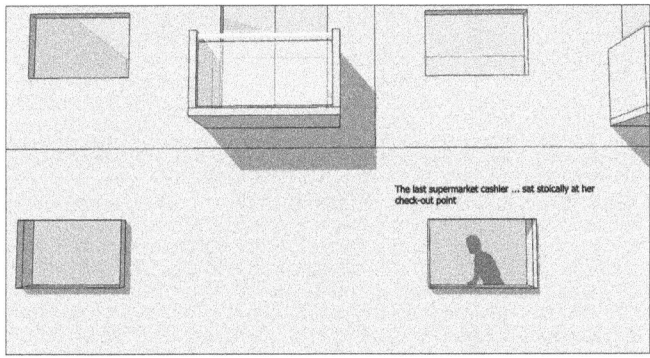

But everyone keeps doing their jobs, and are happy to see the new neighbouring High-Rise beginning to take in residents.

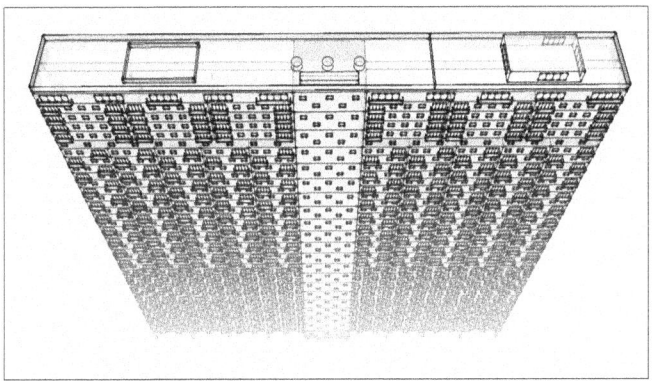

COPING WITH ZERO TO A MILLION DECIMALS:
THE BALLARD BOTS

Thinking Ballard's ideas should naturally have a presence on social media and inspired by an online course in electronic literature by Mark Sample and the Twitterbot code (now sadly non-functional) of Zach Whalen, I created three Twitterbots in 2014:

JG Ballard Openings: which simply published a single sentence from Ballard's published work every day.

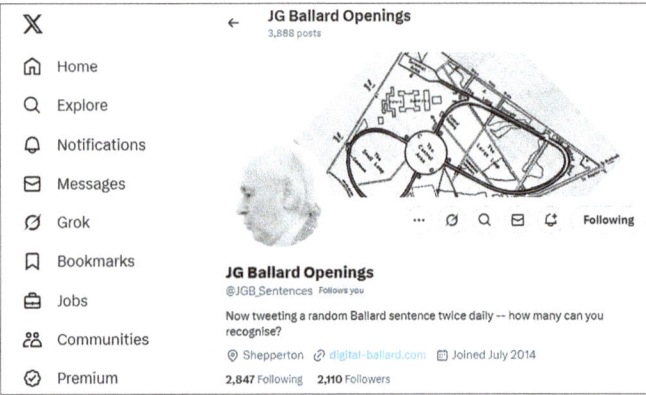

Crash Cutup: which created a mashup sentence from Ballard's novel *Crash* daily.

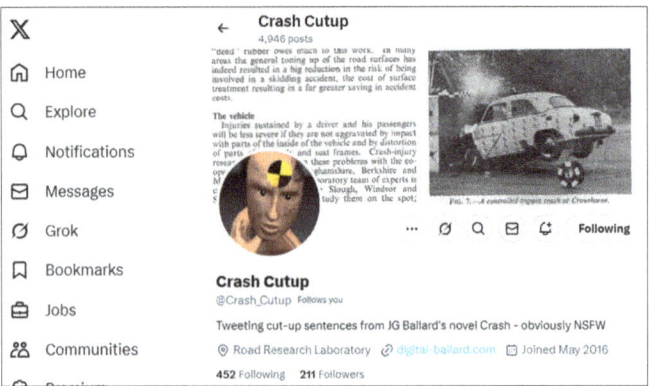

And **New Ballard:** this created Markov Chain sentences trained on Ballard's works: *Crash, Concrete Island* and *High-Rise*.

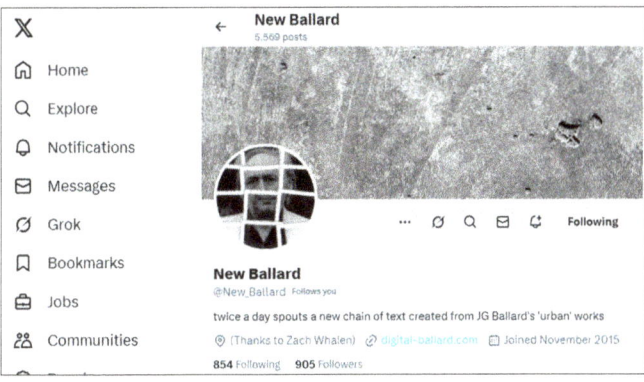

Andrew Wenaus' excellent book *The Literature of Exclusion: Dada, Data and The Threshold of Electronic Literature* (2021), contains an analysis of these bots in relation to Ballard's work. Wenaus says so many interesting things about the subject I'll quote him at length here:

"Ballard's concerns are physical, psychological, and civic. All this lends itself to Mike Bonsall's Digital Ballard, Ballard Twitter bots, and Bonsall's investigation into the ultimate non-space where rogue AI literally can endlessly self-generate and re-permutate: the internet. For Ballard, non-spaces signify the social architecture as an absent referent; the internet only intensifies this nullification. Bonsall explains his Bots and where the idea came from:

> 'Although I haven't had much in the way of formal art education, a series of influences have brought me to where I am with Digital Ballard. I had an early interest in Burroughs' cut-up techniques and Ballard's more experimental writings, and was an early adopter of computer technology (Sinclair ZX Spectrum). It's interesting that both Burroughs and Ballard had computer-oriented friends and collaborators—Ian Sommerville and Christopher

Evans—who both died young, before they could become a lasting influence.

'As well as failing to obtain a medical degree (like Burroughs and Ballard before me), I have worked as an educational technologist, I.T. trainer and analyst at a university, giving me an interest in, and access to, a wide range of computing equipment and software.

Coming of age in the Punk era taught me that you don't need to ask permission, you can just go do it yourself. I've heard the filmmaker Shane Meadows talk of his method in a similar way: "Fast, Fun and Fuck-it." Pete Shelley, who sadly died recently, was a brilliant example of this, setting up gigs, a band and a record label with minimal knowledge but great enthusiasm.

'While a student of the U.K. Open University I took the notorious art course TAD292: Art and Environment. A radical, perhaps even a Situationist, course which opened my eyes to alternative art practices … I was also influenced by the very nature of Ballard's writing, which seems to presuppose another world, just out of sight, that might somehow be reached by an ever-more intense interrogation of the text. As Ballard himself put it: "It's a little as if I were leading the reader to a deserted laboratory, and that I put a collection of specimens and all the necessary equipment at his disposal. It's his job then to relate these elements together and create reactions from them."'

"The Ballardian Twitter bots are an amusing and insightful extension of Ballard's central thesis (that the psyche is both constitutive and constituted by the psychopathology of non-place environments) through automated means. Bonsall's three Ballard Twitter bots are @JGB_Sentences, @Crash_Cutup, and

@New_Ballard. All three offer a progression of significance when considering psychopathy and the media functionalities of the inhuman. (pp 227-8)

"Ballard's prose is always highly calculated, dispassionate, and articulate; Bonsall's BallardBots achieve this functionality to a new inhuman degree. After all, authorship is not the best way to think about the bots at all. Instead, they are self-generated Ballardian characters in a dual sense: first, they are representations of an agent with (or without) identifiable human traits and, second, literal symbols (letters and coded numbers representing data) that regularly reiterate themselves into new sentences and are usable by an algorithm. In this sense, their choices and decisions are not their own but, rather, reactions to an attractive, constitutive, and alterior logic or code. For a Ballardian character, "'decides' is no doubt too active a word," Fisher notes, "in every respect the typical Ballard character ... discovers rather than initiates" and "finds himself drawn into a logic he is compelled to investigate." Bonsall's Twitter bots are the scouts sent ahead--not into shopping malls, airports, or luxury high-rises--but onto the internet to see how the future may unfold according to an inhuman sychopathology of algorithmic culture. Bonsall ultimately establishes a means by which Ballard can operate according to the nihilism at the logical center of an intensified non-place. (pp 231-2)

"Bonsall's BallardBots are something different altogether: they are not virtual subjects, nor are they digital natives. Instead, the bots are procedures, functions set in motion by Bonsall to inhabit Twitter, to be the inhuman scouts on the surface of an otherwise inhuman non-space with seemingly endless fractal iterations. "Cyberspace," after all, Bolter and Grusin write, "is a shopping mall in the ether; it fits smoothly into our contemporary networks of transportation, communication, and economic exchange." (p 234)

"This is not to say that Ballard or Bonsall are anti-humanist (like Wiener, they are not). However, their work examines processes that eschew the triumph of humanist value without evaluating it as such. Yet, both Ballard and Bonsall leave it to the extra-diegetic readerly agent to consider this cyborgian dyshomeostasis without providing further comment on the author's or programmer's behalf. (p 236)

" ... That is, cyber-Ballardian scouts are endlessly testing the water as self-reflexive functions of functionality. When we are not inhabiting Twitter (i.e., not logged on), @JGB_Sentences, @Crash_Cutup, and @New_Ballard are still posting and, we should add, could technically continue to do so ad infinitum (though, in actuality, they will not). Like the Ballardian psychopath, BallardBots are those who endlessly discover and operate according to an endlessly combinatorial logic that merges with the logic of non-space without meaning. In many ways, Bonsall's bots are intensified Ballardianism: self-automated processes qualifying the asemic environments of functional code, able to cope with zero to a million decimals." (p 238)

That final paragraph by Andrew Wenaus was indeed prophetic. The takeover of Twitter and consequent strangling of API access stopped the original twitter bots posting.

On Bluesky I was able to recreate @JGB_Sentences (as @ballardbot.bsky.social) and @Crash_Cutup (as @crash-cutup.bsky.social)

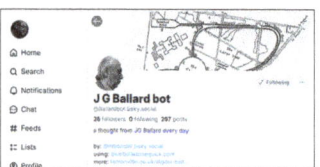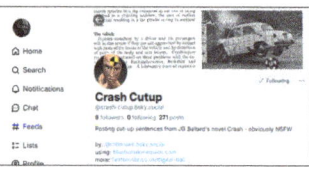

Where I hope they will continue to be "the scouts sent ahead onto the internet to see how the future may unfold according to an inhuman sychopathology of algorithmic culture."

Answers to Ballard in Legoland:

1. *Rushing to Paradise*
2. *The Kindness of Women*
3. *Millennium People*
4. *Super-Cannes*
5. *Cocaine Nights*
6. *The Crystal World*
7. *Crash*
8. *High-Rise*
9. *Kingdom Come*
10. *The Unlimited Dream Company*
11. *Hello America*
12. *The Drowned World*
13. *The Day of Creation*
14. *Running Wild*
15. *Concrete Island*
16. *The Wind From Nowhere*
17. *The Drought*
18. *Empire of the Sun*

Also By The Terminal Press:

The J.G. Ballard Book 2013
Deep Ends: The J.G. Ballard Anthology 2014
Deep Ends: The J.G. Ballard Anthology 2015
Deep Ends: The J.G. Ballard Anthology 2016
Deep Ends: A Ballardian Anthology 2018
Deep Ends: A Ballardian Anthology 2019
Deep Ends: A Ballardian Anthology 2020
Deep Ends: A Ballardian Anthology 2021
Deep Ends: A Ballardian Anthology 2022
Deep Ends: A Ballardian Anthology 2023

Dominika Oramus - Grave New World: The Decline of the West in the Fiction of JG Ballard

Lawrence Russell - Radio Brazil
Lawrence Russell - Outlaw Academic
Lawrence Russell - Temple of the Two Moons

Don McKay - Gambari

Rick McGrath - Straight Man: Rock Star Interviews, Reviews & Photos from the 1970s Underground Press
Rick McGrath - The Disenchanted Forest
Rick McGrath (editor) - Unauthorised Departures

www.ingramcontent.com/pod-product-compliance
Lightning Source LLC
Chambersburg PA
CBHW040517220526
45473CB00012B/2887